GOVERNMENT PROCEDURES AND OPERATIONS

# FEDERAL INSPECTORS GENERAL: OVERVIEW, AUTHORITIES, AND OVERSIGHT ISSUES

# GOVERNMENT PROCEDURES AND OPERATIONS

Additional books in this series can be found on Nova's website under the Series tab.

Additional e-books in this series can be found on Nova's website under the e-book tab.

GOVERNMENT PROCEDURES AND OPERATIONS

# FEDERAL INSPECTORS GENERAL: OVERVIEW, AUTHORITIES, AND OVERSIGHT ISSUES

EMMETT CRUZ
EDITOR

nova publishers
*New York*

**Library of Congress Cataloging-in-Publication Data**

ISBN: 978-1-63485-524-2

*Published by Nova Science Publishers, Inc. † New York*

# CONTENTS

# PREFACE

Federal inspectors general (IGs) are authorized to combat waste, fraud, and abuse within their affiliated federal entities. To execute their missions, offices of inspector general (OIGs) conduct and publish audits and investigations—among other duties. Two major enactments—the Inspector General Act of 1978 and its amendments of 1988 —established federal IGs as permanent, nonpartisan, and independent offices in more than 70 federal agencies. OIGs serve to assist Congress in overseeing executive branch—and a few legislative branch—agencies. They provide recommendations and findings to their affiliated agency head and to Congress that may save the government millions of dollars per year. As a result, Congress may have an interest in ensuring that federal OIGs have the appropriate authorities and access to information they need to perform their investigations, audits, and evaluations. Concurrently, Congress has a responsibility to protect some records and information, such as national security information or information about an ongoing criminal investigation, from improper release. This book provides background on the statutory creation of federal OIGs and provides historical context for contemporary debates about the strengths and limitations of the offices. Furthermore, this book provides context on the role of the Integrity Committee (IC) in investigating allegations of wrongdoing made against employees of the IG community. The book provides analysis of congressional proposals seeking to amend and improve the IC's operations, and includes additional potential policy options for improvement of oversight of the IG community.

In: Federal Inspectors General
Editor: Emmett Cruz

ISBN: 978-1-63485-524-2


*Chapter 1*

# FEDERAL INSPECTORS GENERAL: HISTORY, CHARACTERISTICS, AND RECENT CONGRESSIONAL ACTIONS*

***Wendy Ginsberg and Michael Greene***

## SUMMARY

Federal inspectors general (IGs) are authorized to combat waste, fraud, and abuse within their affiliated federal entities. To execute their missions, offices of inspector general (OIGs) conduct and publish audits and investigations—among other duties. Two major enactments—the Inspector General Act of 1978 and its amendments of 1988 (codified at 5 U.S.C. Appendix)—established federal IGs as permanent, nonpartisan, and independent offices in more than 70 federal agencies.

OIGs serve to assist Congress in overseeing executive branch—and a few legislative branch— agencies. They provide recommendations and findings to their affiliated agency head and to Congress that may save the government millions of dollars per year. As a result, Congress may have an interest in ensuring that federal OIGs have the appropriate authorities and access to information they need to perform their investigations, audits, and evaluations. Concurrently, Congress has a responsibility to protect some records and information, such as national security information or information about an ongoing criminal investigation, from

* This is an edited, reformatted and augmented version of a Congressional Research Service, Publication No. R43814, dated December 8, 2014.

improper release. This report provides background on the statutory creation of federal OIGs and provides historical context for contemporary debates about the strengths and limitations of the offices.

Congress has a number of tools at its disposal to enhance OIG oversight, including through the introduction or passage of legislation, through formal letters to and from overseers, and through oversight hearings. Recent legislative initiatives have enhanced OIG oversight by creating new IGs (H.R. 302 and H.R. 3770, 113$^{th}$ Congress), expanding the authority of existing ones (P.L. 113-6, H.R. 314, 113$^{th}$ Congress), or increasing IGs' reporting requirements to Congress (H.R. 1211, 113$^{th}$ Congress; H.R. 658, 112$^{th}$ Congress).

In August 2014, 47 federal IGs wrote a letter to leadership of the Senate Committee on Homeland Security and Governmental Affairs and the House Committee on Oversight and Government Reform indicating difficulties in acquiring records or other information from the agencies with which they are affiliated. The letter stated that certain agencies' unwillingness to provide requested information represents "potentially serious challenges to the authority of every Inspector General and our ability to conduct our work thoroughly, independently, and in a timely manner." The IGs asked Congress to provide "a strong, generally applicable reaffirmation" of Congress's intentions in the IG Act to require agencies to provide federal OIGs with access to all requested records and information.

In September 2014, the House Committee on Oversight and Government Reform held a hearing at which the IGs from the allegedly unresponsive agencies testified, detailing difficulties in obtaining agency information. All Members at the hearing expressed concerns about the IGs' inability to access requested information.

Strengthening government oversight through IGs and ensuring proper access to agency records, among other issues, will likely continue to be of interest to Congress in the future.

## INTRODUCTION

Congress created federal inspectors general (IGs) to combat waste, fraud, and abuse within designated federal departments and agencies. Generally, these IGs head permanent, nonpartisan, and independent offices that conduct audits, investigations, and other evaluations of federal department and agency programs and operations. Offices of inspectors general (OIGs) exist in more than 70 federal agencies, including all departments and larger agencies, numerous boards and commissions, and other entities.[1]

Federal OIGs date back to the mid-1970s. Since their establishment, they have been granted substantial independence and powers to audit, investigate, and evaluate federal programs and agencies to assist Congress in its oversight duties.[2] In most cases, OIGs produce reports, often made available to the public, that provide findings and recommendations to their affiliated agencies. Often these recommendations find ways to increase federal efficiency or examine allegations of employee misconduct. OIGs are predominantly located in executive branch agencies, but several legislative branch entities—for example, the Library of Congress, the Government Accountability Office, and the Government Printing Office—are also overseen by IGs.

The overwhelming majority of IGs are governed by the Inspector General Act of 1978, as amended (hereinafter referred to as the IG Act).[3] The IG Act structures IG appointments and removals, IG powers and authorities, and IG responsibilities and duties.[4] The law also authorizes and delineates the responsibilities of the Council of the Inspectors General for Integrity and Efficiency (CIGIE), which comprises a vast majority of federal IGs and "works to address integrity, economy, and effectiveness issues that transcend individual [g]overnment agencies" and seeks to "increase the professionalism and effectiveness of [OIG] personnel by developing policies, standards, and approaches to aid in the establishment of a well-trained and highly skilled workforce."[5]

Congress may have an interest in ensuring that federal OIGs have the appropriate authorities and access they need to perform their investigations, audits, and evaluations. Concurrently, Congress has a responsibility to protect from improper release some records and information, such as information related to national security or to ongoing criminal investigations. This report provides background on the statutory creation of federal OIGs and provides historical context for contemporary debates about the strengths and limitations of the offices.

## EVOLUTION OF THE INSPECTOR GENERAL ACT OF 1978

Since its enactment in 1978, the IG Act has been substantially amended twice:

- The Inspector General Act Amendments of 1988 created a new set of IGs in "designated federal entities" (DFEs), which are usually smaller federal agencies.[6] The IG Act of 1988 also added to the reporting obligations of all IGs and agency heads, among other things.

- The Inspector General Reform Act of 2008 established the Council of the Inspectors General for Integrity and Efficiency; amended reporting obligations, salary, bonus, and award provisions; amended removal requirements; and added budget protections—including requiring that Congress be provided IGs' unaltered original budget submissions.[7]

Other laws have established or amended the authorities provided to IGs in specified agencies or programs—either directly under the IG Act or as separate pieces of legislation. Still other enactments have enhanced IG independence or added new responsibilities and powers on a selective basis.[8] As a result, statutory IGs are not identical. In certain cases, differences among IGs are significant. Nonetheless, in general, statutory IGs follow the standards, guidelines, and directives in the IG Act.[9]

Typically, the jurisdiction of an inspector general includes only the programs and operations of a single affiliated agency and its components. A few IGs, however, have express authority to audit and investigate more than one agency, organization, program, or activity.[10]

## TYPES, CATEGORIES, AUTHORITIES, AND OPERATIONS

As noted above, statutory offices of inspector general are currently authorized in more than 70 federal establishments, designated federal entities, and other agencies or programs.[11] Authority for most of the IGs is provided by the IG Act.[12] The statutory IGs may be grouped by these criteria: the method of appointment, the authorizing statute, and the branch of government in which they are located.

In addition to appointment structure, however, IGs can be identified and described using a host of different authorities, requirements, and operations. This section provides an overview of the various similarities and differences among federal IGs.

## Method of Appointment[13]

Generally, there are five different methods of appointment for an IG:

1) appointment by the President with the advice and consent of the Senate, under the IG Act;
2) appointment by the head of the affiliated agency, under the IG Act;
3) appointment by the President with the advice and consent of the Senate, enacted under a separate statutory authority;
4) appointed by the President alone or with the advice and consent of the Senate, enacted under separate statutory authority, and temporary; and
5) appointed by the agency head, enacted under separate statutory authority, and located in the legislative branch.

### *Appointment by the President with the Advice and Consent of the Senate, under the IG Act*

"Federal establishments," as identified in the IG Act, include the 15 Cabinet departments and larger federal agencies. Each IG is appointed by the President with the advice and consent of the Senate and can be removed by the President, but *not* by the agency head.[14]

### *Appointment by the Head of the Affiliated Agency, under the IG Act*

"Designated federal entities" (DFEs), as identified in the IG Act, include the usually smaller boards, commissions, foundations, and government entities. Each IG is appointed by and removable by the head of the affiliated agency.[15]

### *Appointment by the President with the Advice and Consent of the Senate, Enacted under Separate Statutory Authority*

Two other permanent executive agencies operate under their own statutory authorities. These are the Inspector General in the Central Intelligence Agency (P.L. 101-193) and the Inspector General of the Intelligence Community within the Office of the Director of National Intelligence, whose jurisdiction extends across all IC elements or components (P.L. 111-259). Each IG is appointed by the President with the advice and consent of the Senate and is removable by the President, but *not* by the agency head.

***Appointed by the President Alone or with the Advice and Consent of the Senate, Enacted under Separate Statutory Authority, and Temporary***

Two temporary programs operate under their own authorities and reflect different appointment structures.[16] These IGs are the Special Inspector General for Afghanistan Reconstruction (SIGAR), a direct presidential appointee, unique among IGs (P.L. 110-181); and the Special Inspector General for the Troubled Asset Relief Program (SIGTARP), who is appointed by the President with the advice and consent of the Senate (P.L. 110-343).[17]

***Appointed by the Head of the Affiliated Agency, Enacted under Separate Statutory Authority, and Located in the Legislative Branch***

Five legislative branch IGs operate under their own statutory authorities. These are the Architect of the Capitol (P.L. 110-161); Government Accountability Office (P.L. 110-323); Government Printing Office (P.L. 100-504); Library of Congress (P.L. 109-55); and U.S. Capitol Police (P.L. 109-55). Each IG is appointed and removable by the head of the agency.

## Purposes

Pursuant to Section 2 of the IG Act, the three principal purposes of inspectors general who are governed by the IG Act are

- conducting and supervising audits and investigations related to agency programs and operations;
- providing leadership and coordination as well as recommending policies for activities designed to promote the economy, efficiency, and effectiveness of the affiliated agencies' programs and operations; providing for the prevention and detection of fraud and abuse in such programs and operations; and
- keeping the agency head and Congress "fully and currently informed about problems and deficiencies relating to" such programs and the necessity for and "progress of corrective action."[18]

Over time and as conditions dictated, some IGs have acquired unique responsibilities on a selective basis. For instance, the Dodd-Frank Wall Street Reform and Consumer Protection Act contains a number of provisions that add to the duties of IGs over certain federally insured funds. The Dodd-Frank legislation also requires coordination among relevant IGs via a Council of Inspectors General on Financial Oversight.[19]

## Authorities

To carry out their purposes, IGs covered by the IG Act (establishment and DFE) have been granted broad authority to

- conduct audits and investigations;
- access directly the records and information related to the affiliated agency's programs and operations;
- request assistance from other federal, state, and local government agencies;
- subpoena information and documents;
- administer oaths when conducting interviews;
- hire staff and manage their own resources;
- receive and respond to complaints from agency employees, whose identity is to be protected; and
- implement the cash incentive award program in their agency for employee disclosures of waste, fraud, and abuse.[20]

Notwithstanding these broad powers, IGs are *not* authorized to take corrective action themselves. The IG Act prohibits the transfer of "program operating responsibilities" to an IG.[21]

## Reporting Requirements (to the Attorney General, Agency Head, Congress, and the Public)

IGs have various reporting obligations to Congress, the Attorney General, agency heads, and the public. One such obligation is to report suspected violations of federal criminal law directly and expeditiously to the Attorney General.[22] IGs are also required to report semiannually (twice per year) about their activities, findings, and recommendations to the agency head, who must submit the IG's report to Congress within 30 days.[23] The agency head's submission must provide the IG's report unaltered, but it may include any additional comments from the agency head. These semiannual reports are to be made available to the public in another 60 days.[24] IGs are also to report "particularly serious or flagrant problems" immediately to the agency head, who must submit the IG report (unaltered but with his or her comments) to Congress within seven days.[25]

## Independence

IGs have broad powers and protections that support their independence, including the authority to hire their own staff. Their independent status is reinforced in other ways; for instance, many IGs are vested with law enforcement powers.[26] IGs determine the priorities and projects for their offices without outside direction, in most cases. IGs may decide to conduct a review requested by the agency head, President, legislators, employees, or any member of the public; but they are not obligated to do so, unless it is called for in law.[27] Congress, however, has mandated in legislation that OIGs conduct certain reviews. For example, pursuant to the Federal Information Security Act of 2002, federal IGs are required annually to review federal agencies' information technology security programs.[28]

IGs serve under the "general supervision" of the agency head, reporting exclusively to the head or to the officer next in rank if such authority is delegated.[29]

### *Budgets and Appropriations*

Pursuant to the IG Act, presidentially appointed IGs in establishments are provided a separate appropriations account, known colloquially as a "line item," for their offices.[30] This provision prevents agency administrators from limiting, transferring, or otherwise reducing IG funding once it has been specified in law. In contrast, each DFE IG's budget is part of the affiliated entity's budget and may be susceptible to some reallocation of funds.

The Inspector General Reform Act of 2008 amended the budget process for establishment and DFE OIGs. Pursuant to the reform act amendments, OIG budget estimates (i.e., budget proposals, which are to include operations, IG training, and other costs to support the federal IG council)[31] are to be provided to the affiliated agency. The affiliated agency's aggregated budget request to the President is required to include the OIG's original budget estimate and any response from the IG to the agency head's suggested changes. The President, in turn, must then include in his budget submission to Congress

- the IG's original budget estimate;
- the President's requested amounts for the IG; and
- comments of the affected IG, if he or she determines that the President's budget would "substantially inhibit" the IG from performing his or her duties.[32]

Similar provisions apply to the IGs for the CIA and of the IC.[33]

***Appointment, Removal, and Term Limits***

Some variations occur with regard to the appointment and removal of IGs, reflecting, to a degree, the status, location, and permanency of the affiliated agency. All IGs, however, follow certain laws and practices to help ensure impartiality and political nonpartisanship.

Pursuant to the IG Act and other statutes, IGs are to be selected without regard to political affiliation and solely on the basis of integrity and demonstrated ability in accounting, auditing, financial and management analysis, law, public administration, or investigations.[34] IGs that are presidentially appointed with the advice and consent of the Senate can be removed only by the President (or through the impeachment process in Congress).[35]

IGs in designated federal entities and legislative branch agencies vary in appointment structure, removal procedure, and term limits. The DFE IGs are appointed by and can be removed by the agency head, who must notify Congress in writing 30 days in advance when exercising the removal authority.[36] Furthermore, the U.S. Postal Service (USPS) IG is the only inspector general with the restriction that he or she can be removed only "for cause" (e.g., malfeasance or neglect of duty) and then only by the written concurrence of at least seven of the nine presidentially appointed governors of USPS.[37] In other cases, the Dodd-Frank Wall Street Reform and Consumer Protection Act amended the IG Act to require the written concurrence of a two-thirds majority of board or commission members for removal of an IG in any designated federal entity in which the board or commission is considered the DFE head.

## COORDINATION AND CONTROLS

Coordination among the IGs and controls over their actions, which might include investigating charges of wrongdoing by the IGs themselves, exists through several channels—including interagency councils created by public law or administrative directive.

## Council of the Inspectors General for Integrity and Efficiency

Perhaps the most important coordinating body for IGs is the Council of the Inspectors General for Integrity and Efficiency (CIGIE), created by the IG Reform Act of 2008.[38] CIGIE is designed to aid coordination among IGs and maintain one or more academies for the professional training of auditors, investigators, inspectors, evaluators, and other personnel in IG offices.[39] CIGIE includes all statutory IGs along with other relevant officers, such as a representative of the Federal Bureau of Investigation (FBI) and the Special Counsel of the Office of Special Counsel.[40] The council chairperson is an IG chosen from within its ranks, while the executive chairperson is the OMB deputy director of management.[41]

## Other Coordinative Bodies

Other interagency mechanisms have been created by law or administrative directive to assist coordination among IGs. For example, a separate Council of Inspectors General on Financial Oversight—chaired by the Treasury IG and composed of IGs from nine financial agencies—was established by statute to facilitate information sharing among them and develop ways to improve financial oversight.[42] In 2010, Congress enacted a bill requiring the establishment of the Intelligence Community Inspectors General Forum. The forum consists of all statutorily or administratively established inspectors with oversight responsibility of an element of the IC and is chaired by the IC Inspector General.[43] At least two administrative organizations have also been created to help coordinate IG activities and capabilities in selected areas: the Homeland Security Roundtable and the Defense Council on Integrity and Efficiency, composed primarily of the Department of Defense (DOD) audit and investigative units and chaired by the DOD IG.[44]

## Investigation of Alleged OIG Wrongdoing

Investigations of alleged misconduct by OIG officials—including IGs themselves—are the province of a special Integrity Committee within CIGIE.[45] The special committee receives, reviews, and refers for investigation allegations of wrongdoing by these officials, with the relevant processes and procedures spelled out in the IG Act. The committee is composed of four IGs on the council, along with the Special Counsel, the Director of the Office of Government Ethics, and the FBI representative on the council, who chairs the committee.[46]

# Recent Congressional Legislation and Oversight

Congress has the authority to amend the IG Act as well as oversee the operations of IGs and their offices. In recent Congresses, these legislative and oversight authorities have been used in a variety of ways, including through introduction or passage of bills, through formal letters to and from overseers, and through oversight hearings. The section below includes several recent examples of legislation and oversight that sought to amend the IG Act or clarify Congress's position on how the law should be executed.

## Selected Legislation in Recent Congresses

Congress has perennially attempted to address IG oversight through legislation in a number of ways, including expanding an existing IG's oversight to additional federal entities; creating a new IG for an agency that appears to be without such an oversight mechanism; requiring additional reporting measures by one or several IGs; and various other administrative initiatives like ensuring competitive pay rates for IGs.

One example of legislation expanding the jurisdiction of an existing IG is P.L. 113-6 (enacted in the 113$^{th}$ Congress), which established an IG at the Commission on Civil Rights. The law requires the IG at GAO to "also hold the position of Inspector General of the Commission on Civil Rights."[47] The law, among other things, also provided the new commission IG the same responsibilities and authorities as other federal DFE IGs; authorized the use of GAO resources and personnel to perform the commission's IG responsibilities; and created procedures to waive certain reporting requirements required of other federal IGs (pending approval from the House and Senate Committees on Appropriation).

The Inspector General Improvement Act (introduced as H.R. 314 in the 113th Congress and H.R. 6723 in the 112th Congress), is another example of legislative action seeking to amend the responsibilities of existing IGs. Both bills sought to require existing IGs to assume oversight responsibilities of smaller federal entities that appear not to have OIG oversight. For example, H.R. 314 would have required that the U.S. Agency for International Development IG "supervise, direct, and control audit and investigative activities" at the Trade and Development Agency, the Japan-United States Friendship Commission, and the Overseas Private Investment Corporation.[48] Both bills were reported to the House Committee on Oversight and Government Reform. No further action was taken on either bill.

In addition to amending the jurisdiction of existing IGs to oversee the operations of certain federal entities, Congress has, from time to time, proposed legislation seeking to create an entirely new IG. For example, The Metropolitan Washington Airports Authority Inspector General Act of 2013 (H.R. 302, 113th Congress) sought to establish an IG for the Metropolitan Washington Airports Authority (MWAA), which "operates a two-airport system that provides domestic and international air service for the mid-Atlantic region."[49] In another example, the Bureau of Consumer Financial Protection-Inspector General Reform Act of 2013 (H.R. 3770, 113th Congress), among other requirements, sought to create a new, separate "federal establishment" IG to audit, investigate, and evaluate the CFPB. The bill would have also required the CFPB IG to appear before several congressional committees two times per year to present the contents of the OIG's statutorily required semi-annual reports. Pursuant to Section 3(c) of H.R. 3770, 2% of the CFPB's annual funding would have been provided to the OIG. The bill would have also required the President to appoint the CFPB's IG within 60 days of enactment.[50]

There have been a number of legislative efforts by Congress in recent years to place additional reporting requirement on all IGs, certain IGs, or one particular IG. For example, the FOIA Act (H.R. 1211, 113th Congress), would have required IGs government-wide to review their affiliated agency's compliance with the Freedom of Information Act (FOIA).[51] The Reducing Over-Classification Act (H.R. 553, enacted in the 111th Congress), among other provisions, required certain IGs to evaluate whether agencies are appropriately applying classification policies and to "identify policies, procedures, rules, regulations, or management practices that may be contributing to persistent misclassification."[52] The FAA Modernization and Reform Act of 2012 (H.R. 658, enacted in the 112th Congress), among other provisions, required the Department of Transportation's IG to report to Congress each fiscal year from 2013 to 2015 on "the number of new small business concerns owned and controlled by socially and economically disadvantaged individuals," including veterans, that participated in certain Federal Aviation Administration programs.[53]

Other bills may address several IG-community related issues. In the 113th Congress, for example, the Oversight Workforce Improvement Act of 2014 (S. 1953), among other things, sought to codify the pay rates of IGs at designated federal entities and would have statutorily required the IG of the Intelligence Community and the IG of the Central Intelligence Agency (CIA) to be members of CIGIE. Section 4 of S. 1953 sought to set the average pay of an IG at a designated federal entity as "no less than the average total compensation (including bonuses)" of the affiliated agency's "senior level officials," which include the "General Counsel, Chief Information Officer, Chief Financial Officer, Chief Human Capital Officer, or Chief Acquisition Officer." The bill would have provided CIGIE the authority to investigate allegations of wrongdoing made against an IG's special counsel or deputy special counsel.[54] Currently, as noted above, CIGIE has the authority to investigate allegations of wrongdoing against only an IG or certain members of the IG's staff. S. 1953 was referred to the Senate Committee on Homeland Security and Governmental Affairs. No further action has been taken on the bill.

## Selected Recent Congressional Hearings

In addition to introducing legislation related to federal IGs, some congressional committees have held hearings that examine IG-related issues. For example, in November 2013, the Senate Committee on Homeland Security and Governmental Affairs' Subcommittee on Efficiency and Effectiveness of Federal Programs and Federal Workforce held a hearing entitled *Strengthening Government Oversight: Examining the Roles and Effectiveness of Oversight Positions Within the Federal Workforce*.[55]

At the hearing, two federal IGs—one from the U.S. Small Business Administration (SBA) and another from the U.S. Department of Justice—provided testimony on the status and limitations of federal IGs.[56] Among the issues raised by Peggy Gustafson, the SBA IG who also testified on behalf of CIGIE, was a suggestion to exempt federal IGs from the Computer Matching and Privacy Protection Act.[57] According to Ms. Gustafson, exempting IGs from the act would allow some IGs "to identify those who improperly receive Federal assistance and payments and subsequently, seek removal of those persons from the program after verification of this information and due process is applied."[58] Ms. Gustafson also stated that IGs may need to be exempted from the Paperwork Reduction Act (PRA),[59] which requires agencies to acquire approval from the Office of Management and Budget (OMB) prior to surveying a particular community or seeking feedback from the public in certain cases. An exemption from the PRA, according to Ms. Gustafson, "would enhance our independence and remove lengthy processes that are hampering our ability to do our job."[60]

At a September 10, 2014, hearing before the House Committee on Oversight and Government Reform, three inspectors general testified to difficulties accessing records and information from their affiliated agencies.[61] The hearing followed the committee's receipt of a letter signed by 47 federal IGs detailing difficulties of IGs accessing requested records from three particular federal agencies: the Peace Corps, the Chemical Safety and Hazard Investigation Board,[62] and the Department of Justice. Pursuant to Section 6(a) of the IG Act, federal IGs are "to have access to all records, reports, audits, reviews, documents, papers, recommendations, or other material available to the applicable establishment which relate to programs and operations with respect to which that Inspector General has responsibilities under this Act." According to the IGs affiliated with the three agencies listed above, the agencies either stalled in providing or did not provide information or records that the IGs requested. According to the Peace Corps IG, for example, the Peace Corps declined to provide the IG with records related to sexual assault victims who were Peace Corps volunteers. The IG testified that the agency's general counsel had asserted that the Kate Puzy Volunteer Protection Act of 2011,[63] which protects the release of certain personally identifiable information about sexual assault victims from being shared beyond "specified individuals," prevents the agency from providing the records to the IG.

# APPENDIX. OFFICES OF INSPECTORS GENERAL AND THEIR AUTHORIZING STATUTES

This appendix provides information about federal inspectors general, past and present, including the years of their establishment, their appointment structures, and tallies of the various types of IGs.

**Table A-1. Statutes Authorizing IGs Appointed by the President with the Advice and Consent of the Senate, 1976-Present (sunset offices in *italics*)**

| Year | Statute | IG Established |
|---|---|---|
| 1976 | P.L. 94-505 | Health, Education, and Welfare (now Health and Human Services; HHS) |
| 1977 | P.L. 95-91 | Energy (DOE) |
| 1978 | P.L. 95-452 | Agriculture (USDA) |
| | | Commerce (DOC) |
| | | Community Services Administration (CSA) |
| | | Housing and Urban Development (HUD) |
| | | Interior (DOI) |
| | | Labor (DOL) |
| | | Transportation (DOT) |
| | | Environmental Protection Agency (EPA) |
| | | General Services Administration (GSA) |
| | | National Aeronautics and Space Administration (NASA) |
| | | Small Business Administration (SBA) |
| | | Veterans Administration (now the Veterans Affairs Department) |
| 1979 | P.L. 96-88 | Education (ED) |
| 1980 | P.L. 96-294 | U.S. Synthetic Fuels Corporation (USSFC) |
| 1980 | P.L. 96-465 | State[a] |
| 1981 | P.L. 97-113 | Agency for International Development (USAID)[b] |
| 1982 | P.L. 97-252 | Defense (DOD) |
| 1983 | P.L. 98-76 | Railroad Retirement Board (RRB) |
| 1986 | P.L. 99-399 | U.S. Information Agency (USIA) |
| 1987 | P.L. 100-213 | Arms Control and Disarmament Agency (ACDA) |
| 1988 | P.L. 100-504 | Justice (DOJ)[c] |
| | | Treasury |
| | | Federal Emergency Management Agency (FEMA)[d] |
| | | Nuclear Regulatory Commission (NRC) |
| | | Office of Personnel Management (OPM) |
| 1989 | P.L. 101-73 | *Resolution Trust Corporation (RTC)* |

**Table A-1. (Continued)**

| Year | Statute | IG Established |
|---|---|---|
| 1989 | P.L. 101-193 | Central Intelligence Agency (CIA)[e] |
| 1993 | P.L. 103-82 | Corporation for National and Community Service (CNCS) |
| 1993 | P.L. 103-204 | Federal Deposit Insurance Corporation (FDIC) |
| 1994 | P.L. 103-296 | Social Security Administration (SSA) |
| 1994 | P.L. 103-325 | *Community Development Financial Institutions Fund (CDFIF)* |
| 1998 | P.L. 105-206 | Treasury Inspector General for Tax Administration (TIGTA)[f] |
| 2000 | P.L. 106-422 | Tennessee Valley Authority (TVA)[g] |
| 2002 | P.L. 107-189 | Export-Import Bank (EXIM) |
| 2002 | P.L. 107-296 | Homeland Security (DHS) |
| 2008 | P.L. 110-289 | Federal Housing Finance Agency (FHFA)[h] |
| 2010 | P.L. 111-259 | Office of Director of National Intelligence (ODNI)[e,i] |

[a] The State Department IG had also served as the IG for ACDA. In 1998, P.L. 105-277 transferred the functions of ACDA and USIA to the State Department and placed the Broadcasting Board of Governors and the International Broadcasting Bureau under the jurisdiction of the State IG.

[b] The USAID IG may also conduct reviews, investigations, and inspections of the Overseas Private Investment Corporation (22 U.S.C. §2199(e)).

[c] In 2002, P.L. 107-273 expanded the jurisdiction of the Department of Justice IG to cover all department components.

[d] P.L. 107-296, which established the Department of Homeland Security (DHS), transferred FEMA's OIG functions to the DHS IG.

[e] All except the CIA and the ODNI IGs are established by and operate under the 1978 Inspector General Act, as amended.

[f] The OIG for Tax Administration in Treasury is the only case where a separate establishment IG, under the 1978 IG Act, exists within an establishment or entity that is otherwise covered by its own statutory IG.

[g] P.L. 106-422, which re-designated the TVA as an establishment, also created, in the Treasury Department, a Criminal Investigator Academy to train IG staff and an Inspector General Forensic Laboratory.

[h] In 1989, P.L. 101-73 abolished the Federal Home Loan Bank Board and placed the new Federal Housing Finance Board under the 1988 IG Act. Both of these predecessor agencies to the Federal Housing Finance Agency were designated federal agencies whose inspectors general were appointed by their agency head.

[i] Prior to the statutory establishment of the ODNI IG as a presidential appointment with the advice and consent of the Senate, P.L. 108-458 granted the Director of National Intelligence (DNI) full discretion to create and construct an OIG in his office (based on provisions in the IG Act). The director created an IG using this administrative authority in 2006. ODNI, *Report on the Progress of the DNI in Implementing "the Intelligence Reform Act of 2004,"* May 2006; and House Select Committee on Intelligence, *Intelligence Authorization Act for FY 2007* (H.Rept. 109-411).

**Table A-2. Designated Federal Entities and Other Agencies with Statutory IGs Appointed by the Head of the Entity or Agency (sunset offices in *italics*)**

| | |
|---|---|
| Action[a] | Government Printing Office (GPO)[b] |
| Amtrak | Interstate Commerce Commission (ICC)[c] |
| Appalachian Regional Commission (ARC) | Legal Services Corporation (LSC) |
| Architect of the Capitol (AOC)[b,d] | Library of Congress (LOC)[b,e] |
| Board of Governors, Federal Reserve System | National Archives and Records Administration (NARA) |
| Board for International Broadcasting (BIB)[f] | National Credit Union Administration (NCUA) |
| Coalition Provisional Authority (in Iraq) (CPA)[b] | National Endowment for the Arts (NEA) |
| Commodity Futures Trading Commission (CFTC) | National Endowment for the Humanities (NEH) |
| Consumer Product Safety Commission (CPSC) | National Geospatial-Intelligence Agency (NGIA)[g] |
| Corporation for Public Broadcasting (CPB) | National Labor Relations Board (NLRB) |
| Defense Intelligence Agency (DIA)[g] | National Reconnaissance Office (NRO)[g] |
| Denali Commission[h] | National Science Foundation (NSF) |
| Election Assistance Commission (EAC)[i] | National Security Agency (NSA)[g] |
| Equal Employment Opportunity Commission (EEOC) | Panama Canal Commission (PCC)[j] |
| Farm Credit Administration (FCA) | Peace Corps (PC) |
| Federal Communications Commission (FCC) | Pension Benefit Guaranty Corporation (PBGC) |
| Federal Deposit Insurance Corporation (FDIC)[k] | Postal Regulatory Commission (PRC)[l] |
| Federal Election Commission (FEC) | Securities and Exchange Commission (SEC) |
| Federal Home Loan Bank Board (FHLBB)[m] | Smithsonian Institution |
| Federal Housing Finance Board (FHFB)[m] | Special Inspector General for Iraq Reconstruction (SIGIR)[b] |
| Federal Labor Relations Authority (FLRA) | Tennessee Valley Authority (TVA)[n] |
| Federal Maritime Commission (FMC) | U.S. Capitol Police[b,e] |
| Federal Trade Commission (FTC) | U.S. International Trade Commission |
| Government Accountability Office (GAO)[b,o] | U.S. Postal Service[p] |

Notes: This table does not include the Special Inspector General for Afghanistan Reconstruction who is appointed by the President alone (P.L. 110-181, §1229; 122 Stat. 379).

[a] In 1993, P.L. 103-82 merged Action into the new Corporation for National and Community Service.

[b] All agencies listed in this table—except SIGIR, AOC, GAO, GPO, LOC, and the U.S. Capitol Police—are considered "designated federal entities" (DFEs) and placed directly under the 1978 IG Act, as amended. Coalition Provisional Authority was dissolved in mid-2004, with its IG converted to SIGIR.

[c] The ICC was abolished in 1995 by P.L. 104-88.

[d] P.L. 110-161, Consolidated Appropriations Act for FY2008, Division H.

[e] The Legislative Branch Appropriations Act, FY2006 (P.L. 109-55) added IGs to LOC and the Capitol Police, whose IG has specialized responsibilities.

[f] The Board for International Broadcasting was abolished by P.L. 103-236 and its functions transferred to the International Broadcasting Bureau within USIA, which also was abolished and its functions transferred to the State Department.

[g] P.L. 111-259, Intelligence Authorization Act for Fiscal Year 2010, §431(a).

[h] P.L. 105-277 (42 U.S.C. 3121), Denali Commission Act of 1998, as amended.

[i] P.L. 107-252, the Help America Vote Act of 2002.

[j] The Panama Canal Commission was ended with the transfer of the Canal to Panama (22 U.S.C. 3611).

[k] In 1993, P.L. 103-204 made the IG in Federal Deposit Insurance Corporation a presidential appointee, subject to Senate confirmation.

[l] P.L. 109-435, §605(a).

[m] In 1989, P.L. 101-73 abolished the Federal Home Loan Bank Board and placed the new Federal Housing Finance Board under the 1988 IG Act.

[n] P.L. 106-422 re-designated TVA as a federal establishment.

[o] P.L. 110-323, §5.

[p] In 1996, the U.S. Postal Service Inspector General post was separated from the Chief Postal Inspector. The separated IG is appointed by, and can be removed only by, the governors.

## Table A-3. Tabulation of Existing Federal Establishments, Entities, or Agencies with IGs Authorized in Law

| Controlling Statutes | President Nominates, Senate Confirms | Agency or Entity Head Appoints | President Appoints | Total |
|---|---|---|---|---|
| 1978 IG Act, as amended | 30 | 33 | 0 | 63 |
| Other statutes | 2[a] | 6[b] | 1[c] | 9 |
| Total | 32 | 39 | 1 | 72 |

[a] The CIA IG and the Special Inspector General for the Troubled Asset Relief Program are appointed by the President with Senate confirmation.

[b] AOC, GAO, GPO, LOC, ODNI, and the U.S. Capitol Police are appointed by agency heads.

[c] The Special Inspector General for Afghanistan Reconstruction is appointed by the President alone and does not require Senate confirmation (P.L. 110-181, §1229; 122 Stat. 379).

## End Notes

[1] Three other inspector general posts (in the armed forces departments) are recognized in public law: Air Force (10 U.S.C. §8020), Army (10 U.S.C. §3020), and Navy (10 U.S.C. §5020). These offices, however, are not examined here, because they have a significantly different heritage, set of authorities, operational structure and organization, and degree of independence.

[2] For more information about congressional oversight tools and options, see CRS Report RL30240, *Congressional Oversight Manual*, by Todd Garvey et al.

[3] 5 U.S.C. (IG Act) Appendix.

[4] The IG Act of 1978, as amended, establishes offices of inspectors general in many federal agencies as well as defines the IG as the head of each of these offices. The act assigns to the IG specific duties and authorities, including the authority "to select, appoint, and employ such officers and employees as may be necessary for carrying out the functions, powers, and duties of the Office." (5 U.S.C. (IG Act) Appendix §6(a)(7)).

[5] Council of the Inspectors General for Integrity and Efficiency, "Mission and Organization," at http://www.ignet.gov/ cigie1.html.

[6] P.L. 100-504.

[7] P.L. 110-409.

[8] For instance, the inspectors general of federal banking agencies and of the Federal Reserve System had been given review and reporting mandates in separate legislation (12 U.S.C. §1831o(k) and 12 U.S.C. §1790d(j), respectively), which were modified in 2010 by the Dodd-Frank Wall Street Reform and Consumer Protection Act (P.L. 111-203, §§987(a) and 988(a)).

[9] OIGs may follow additional regulations, policies, or standards in addition to the IG Act. For example, the Council of the Inspectors General on Integrity and Efficiency maintains "Quality Standards for Inspection and Evaluation," which, pursuant to 5 U.S.C. (IG Act) Appendix §4(b)(1)(A), all OIG employees are required to follow when conducting inspections or evaluations. Available at http://www.ignet.gov/pande/standards/iestds12r.pdf.

[10] 5 U.S.C. (IG Act) Appendix §§2-4 and 8G(g)(1). The Inspector General of the Intelligence Community (IC), created by the Intelligence Authorization Act for Fiscal Year 2010 (P.L. 111-259, §405), has express cross-agency jurisdiction; this enactment recognizes the continued authority of the existing statutory inspectors general over IC components. The same law (P.L. 111-259, §431) created inspector general posts in four Defense Department agencies, identified as "designated federal entities" under the IG Act: the Defense Intelligence Agency, National Geospatial-Intelligence Agency, National Reconnaissance Office, and National Security Agency. The Inspector General of the Department of State and Broadcasting Board of Governors' jurisdiction includes both the Department of State and the Broadcasting Board of Governors (recognizing the Broadcasting Board of Governors as a separate organization outside the State Department; P.L. 105-277, Division G, Title XIII, Chapter 3, §1322(a)(3); 112 Stat. 2681-777 and 2681-778). In 2010, the Inspector General of the Board of Governors for the Federal Reserve System was given jurisdiction over a new organization—the Bureau of Consumer Financial Protection, which was established as an "independent bureau" in the Federal Reserve System by the Dodd-Frank Wall Street Reform and Consumer Protection Act (P.L. 111-203, §1011). To reflect this expanded coverage, the IG was retitled the Inspector General of the Board of Governors of the Federal Reserve System and the Bureau of Consumer Financial Protection (P.L. 111-203, §1081(1)-(2)). Most recently, P.L. 113-6, enacted on March 26, 2013, requires, among

other things, the Government Accountability Office (GAO) IG to concurrently serve as the IG for the Commission on Civil Rights (P.L. 113-6; 127 Stat. 266).

[11] Some now-defunct statutory IGs have been abolished, sunset, or transferred either in tandem with their affiliated agency or when superseded by another inspector general office. The most recent example of the sunset of an IG was the Special Inspector General for Iraq Reconstruction (SIGIR), established by the Emergency Supplemental Appropriations Act for Defense and for the Reconstruction of Iraq and Afghanistan, as amended (P.L. 108-106). SIGIR was abolished in October 2013. SIGIR's final report, which anticipates its abolition, is available from the IG's archived website here: http://cybercemetery.unt.edu/archive/sigir/20131001092420/http://www.sigir.mil/files/quarterlyreports/September2013/Report_-_September_2013.pdf#view=fit. An example of transferred IG responsibilities is the Office of Inspector General in the Office of the Director of National Intelligence (ODNI)—which operated under the full discretionary authority of the Director of National Intelligence (P.L. 108-458). The ODNI IG was supplanted by the Inspector General of the Intelligence Community (IC); the new IC IG post was established by the Intelligence Authorization Act of 2010 (P.L. 111-259, §405) with substantially broader authority, jurisdiction, and independence than the previous IG.

[12] Nine other IGs have been established by and are governed by separate statutes. Seven of the nine are the Inspector General in the Central Intelligence Agency (CIA), the Inspector General of the Intelligence Community within the Office of the Director of National Intelligence (ODNI) with cross-agency jurisdiction, and the inspector general in each of five legislative branch agencies. The other two IGs are the Special Inspector General for Afghanistan Reconstruction and the Special Inspector General for the Trouble Asset Relief Program.

[13] The Appendix contains several tables that detail the establishing legislation and appointment structures of federal IGs.

[14] 5 U.S.C. (IG Act) Appendix, §2. For a listing of IGs in federal establishments, see U.S. Government Accountability Office, *Inspectors General: Reporting on Independence, Effectiveness, and Expertise*, GAO-11-770, September 2011, p. 21, at http://www.gao.gov/assets/330/323642.pdf.

[15] For a listing of IGs in DFEs, see U.S. Government Accountability Office, *Inspectors General: Reporting on Independence, Effectiveness, and Expertise*, p. 22.

[16] A third, temporary special IG, SIGIR, was abolished in October 2013. See supra note 10.

[17] The Troubled Asset Relief Program investment authority expired on October 3, 2010. The termination of that authority did not affect the Treasury Department's ability to administer existing troubled asset purchases and guarantees and its ability to expend TARP funds for obligations entered into before the closing date. Consequently, SIGTARP's oversight mandate did not end. Rather, the special inspector general is authorized to carry out the office's duties until the Government has sold or transferred all assets and terminated all insurance contracts acquired under TARP. See SIGTARP, *Quarterly Report to Congress*, July 25, 2012, p. 15.

[18] DFE IGs and IGs not covered by the IG Act generally have similar or identical purposes, although some IG missions may vary pursuant to their statutory requirements and authorities.

[19] P.L. 111-203, §§989E(a)-989E(b).

[20] 5 U.S.C. (IG Act) Appendix §§6(a), 6(e), and 7; 5 U.S.C. §4512. IGs not explicitly covered by the IG Act may have similar or identical authorities, although some IGs may have additional authorities or be prohibited from exercising the authorities listed here.

[21] 5 U.S.C. (IG Act) Appendix §8G(b) and §9(a)(2). One rationale for this proscription is that it would be difficult, if not impossible, for IGs to audit or investigate programs and operations impartially and objectively if they were directly involved in carrying them out.

[22] 5 U.S.C. (IG Act) Appendix §4(d).

[23] 5 U.S.C. (IG Act) Appendix §5(a), (b).

[24] 5 U.S.C. (IG Act) Appendix §5(c).

[25] 5 U.S.C. (IG Act) Appendix §5(d). IGs are to keep the agency head and Congress "fully and currently informed" by means of the required reports and "otherwise." (5 U.S.C. (IG Act) Appendix §4(a)(5)).

[26] 5 U.S.C. (IG Act) Appendix §§6(a)(4) and 6(e). For more information, see CRS Report R43722, *Offices of Inspectors General and Law Enforcement Authority: In Brief*, by Wendy Ginsberg.

[27] Pursuant to the IG Act, the heads of six agencies—the Departments of Defense, Homeland Security, Justice, and Treasury, plus the U.S. Postal Service and Federal Reserve Board—may prevent or halt the IG from initiating, carrying out, or completing an audit or investigation, or issuing a subpoena, and then only for certain reasons: to preserve national security interests or to protect ongoing criminal investigations, among a few others. (U.S.C. (IG Act) Appendix §§8, 8D(a), 8E(a), 8G(f), 8G(g)(3), and 8I(a)). When exercising this power, the IG Act generally provides for congressional notification of the exercise of such authority, either via the agency head or the inspector general, who must transmit an explanatory statement for such action to specified congressional committees within 30 days. 5 U.S.C. (IG Act) Appendix §§8(b)(3)-8(b)(4) states that the Secretary of Defense must "submit a statement concerning" the exercise of such power to various congressional committees within 30 days and must also submit a "statement of the reasons for the exercise of power" to the congressional committees within an additional 30 days after the submission of the first statement. See also 5 U.S.C. (IG Act) Appendix §8E(a)(2), which requires the Attorney General to notify the IG in writing of the exercise of such power and mandating that the IG transmit a copy of such notice to certain congressional committees.

[28] 44 U.S.C. §3541.

[29] 5 U.S.C. (IG Act) Appendix §§3(a), 8G(d).

[30] 31 U.S.C. §1105(a)(25). The IGs in the CIA and of the IC have similar safeguards for their budget accounts. (50 U.S.C. §3517(f) and 50 U.S.C. §3033(m), respectively.)

[31] The federal IG council, known as the Council of the Inspectors General for Integrity and Efficiency (CIGIE), will be discussed below in greater detail.

[32] 5 U.S.C. (IG Act) Appendix §6(f)(1)-(3).

[33] 50 U.S.C. §3517(f) and 50 U.S.C. §3033(n), respectively.

[34] 5 U.S.C. Appendix (IG Act) §§3(a) and 8G(c). The CIA IG and the IC IG, who operate under different statutes, are to be selected under these criteria as well as prior experience in the field of foreign intelligence or national security and in compliance with the relevant security standards (50 U.S.C. §3517(b) and §3033(c), respectively, for the CIA IG and the IC IG).

[35] 5 U.S.C. Appendix (IG Act) §3. When exercising removal authority, the President must communicate the reasons to Congress in writing 30 days prior to the scheduled removal date. This advance notice allows the inspector general, Congress, or other interested parties to examine and possibly object to the planned removal (5 U.S.C. Appendix §3(b) for presidentially appointed, Senate-confirmed (PAS) IGs under the IG Act; 50 U.S.C. §3517(b)(6) for the IG in the CIA; and 50 U.S.C. §3033(c)(4)) for the IG of the IC).

[36] 5 U.S.C. Appendix (IG Act) §8G(c) and (e). Differences, however, arise over who might be considered to be the "head of the agency" in a DFE. The agency head may be an individual

serving as the administrator or director or as spelled out in law (e.g., the Archivist of the United States in the National Archives and Records Administration), the chairperson of a board or commission, a full board or council as specified in law (e.g., the National Council on the Arts in the National Endowment of the Arts), or a certain super-majority of a governing board. (5 U.S.C. Appendix (IG Act) §§8G(f)(1)-(2) and (4)). In the United States Postal Service (USPS), for instance, the governors appoint the IG.

[37] 39 U.S.C. §202(e)(3).

[38] 5 U.S.C. Appendix (IG Act) §11.

[39] 5 U.S.C. Appendix (IG Act) §11(c)(1)(E).

[40] 5 U.S.C. Appendix (IG Act) §11(b)(1).

[41] 5 U.S.C. Appendix (IG Act) §11(b)(2).

[42] P.L. 111-203, §989E. The members of the Council of Inspectors General on Financial Oversight are the Inspector General of the Board of Governors of the Federal Reserve System; Inspector General of the Commodity Futures Trading Commission; Inspector General of the Department of Housing and Urban Development; Inspector General of the Department of the Treasury (serves as chairperson); Inspector General of the Federal Deposit Insurance Corporation; Inspector General of the Federal Housing Finance Agency; Inspector General of the National Credit Union Administration; Inspector General of the Securities and Exchange Commission; and Special Inspector General for the Troubled Asset Relief Program (until termination of authority).

[43] P.L. 111-259, §405; 50 U.S.C. §403-3h(h).

[44] Office of Inspector General, Department of Defense, *Defense Council on Integrity and Efficiency: Charter*, at http://www.dodig.mil/dcie.html.

[45] 5 U.S.C. Appendix (IG Act) §11(d)(1). Pursuant to the 5 U.S.C. Appendix (IG Act) §11(d)(4)(B), the Integrity Committee has the authority to receive, review, and refer allegations of wrongdoing by the IG or any "staff member" who reports directly to the IG. Additionally, the IG Act authorizes the Integrity Committee to receive, review, and refer allegations of wrongdoing against any employee who holds a position designated by the IG as qualifying as a "staff member." The IG is required to annually submit to the chairperson of the Integrity Committee a list of "positions whose holders are staff members." (5 U.S.C. Appendix §11(d)(4)(B)).

[46] 5 U.S.C. Appendix §11(d)(2).

[47] P.L. 113-6; 127 Stat. 266.

[48] H.R. 314, §2.

[49] Metropolitan Washington Airports Authority, "About the Authority," at http://www.metwashairports.com/263.htm. Currently, the Department of Transportation (DOT) IG has been conducting audits and investigations of the MWAA's activities. DOT was provided explicit statutory authority to perform audits, investigations, and other IG functions for the MWAA in the 2014 Omnibus Appropriations Bill (P.L. 113-76; 128 Stat 600). H.R. 302 would create a new IG with oversight authority exclusively over the MWAA.

[50] The appointment process of a "federal establishment" IG includes the advice and consent of the Senate. Whether the Senate would be required to act within the 60-day time cap to allow for completion of the appointment process is unclear. CFPB and the Board of Governors of the Federal Reserve System are currently overseen jointly by the same IG. H.R. 3770 would have kept this structure in place until a new CFPB IG was appointed and confirmed, resulting in separate IGs for CFPB and the Federal Reserve Board.

[51] FOIA requires agencies to release federal records that are requested by any member of the public, unless those records fit within any one of nine specific statutory exemptions from public release. For more information on FOIA, see CRS Report R41933, *The Freedom of Information Act (FOIA): Background, Legislation, and Policy Issues*, by Wendy Ginsberg.

[52] P.L. 111-258, §6(b); 124 Stat. 2651.

[53] P.L. 112-95, §140(c); 126 Stat. 28.

[54] *Special Counsel* is defined in 5 U.S.C. §1211.

[55] U.S. Congress, Senate Committee on Homeland Security and Governmental Affairs, Subcommittee on the Efficiency and Effectiveness of Federal Programs and the Federal Workforce, *Strengthening Government Oversight: Examining the Roles and Effectiveness of Oversight Positions Within the Federal Workforce*, 113th Cong., 1st sess., November 19, 2013, at http://www.hsgac.senate.gov/subcommittees/fpfw/hearings/strengthening-government-oversight-examiningthe-roles-and-effectiveness-of-oversight-positions-within-the-federal-workforce.

[56] U.S. Congress, House Committee on Oversight and Government Reform, *Obstructing Oversight: Concerns from Inspectors General*, 113th Cong., 2nd sess., September 10, 2014, at http://oversight.house.gov/hearing/obstructingoversight-concerns-inspectors-general/.

[57] 5 U.S.C. §552a.

[58] U.S. Congress, Senate Committee on Homeland Security and Governmental Affairs, Subcommittee on the Efficiency and Effectiveness of Federal Programs and the Federal Workforce, *Strengthening Government Oversight: Examining the Roles and Effectiveness of Oversight Positions Within the Federal Workforce*, 113th Cong., 1st sess., November 19, 2013, S.Hrg. 113-367 (Washington: GPO, 2014), p. 5.

[59] PRA; P.L. 96-511; 44 U.S.C. §§3501-3521. For more information on the PRA see CRS Report R40636, *Paperwork Reduction Act (PRA): OMB and Agency Responsibilities and Burden Estimates*, by Curtis W. Copeland and Vanessa K. Burrows. The authors of that report have left CRS. Questions about its content can be directed to Maeve P. Carey, Analyst in Government Organization and Management.

[60] Ibid., p. 6.

[61] U.S. Congress, House Committee on Oversight and Government Reform, *Obstructing Oversight: Concerns from Inspectors General*, 113th Cong., 2nd Sess., September 10, 2014, at http://oversight.house.gov/hearing/obstructingoversight-concerns-inspectors-general/.

[62] The IG affiliated with the Chemical Safety and Hazard Investigation Board is the Environmental Protection Agency IG.

[63] P.L. 112-57.

In: Federal Inspectors General
Editor: Emmett Cruz

ISBN: 978-1-63485-524-2


*Chapter 2*

# OFFICES OF INSPECTORS GENERAL AND LAW ENFORCEMENT AUTHORITY: IN BRIEF*

*Wendy Ginsberg*

## SUMMARY

Federal inspectors general (IGs) have been granted substantial independence and powers to combat waste, fraud, and abuse within designated federal departments and agencies. To execute their missions, offices of inspector general (OIGs) conduct and publish audits and investigations—among other duties. Established by public law as permanent, nonpartisan, and independent offices, OIGs exist in more than 70 federal agencies, including all departments and larger agencies, along with numerous boards and commissions and other entities. Many OIGs have been vested with law enforcement authority to assist their investigations.

This report provides background on federal offices of inspectors general and their law enforcement authorities in investigations.

In this report, law enforcement authority is generally defined as having the legal authority to

---

* This is an edited, reformatted and augmented version of a Congressional Research Service publication R43722, prepared for Members and Committees of Congress, dated September 8, 2014.

- carry a firearm while engaged in official duties;
- make an arrest without a warrant while engaged in official duties; and
- seek and execute warrants for arrest, search of premises, or seizure of evidence.

This report identifies the laws and regulations that vest certain OIGs with law enforcement authority, which permits the use of guns and ammunition. This report also describes some of the requirements and expectations of OIGs that have law enforcement authority, and includes some reasons that OIGs have expressed a need for law enforcement authority.

## INTRODUCTION

Federal inspectors general (IGs) have been granted substantial independence and powers to combat waste, fraud, and abuse within designated federal departments and agencies. To execute their missions, offices of inspector general (OIGs) conduct and publish audits and investigations—among other duties.

In some cases, employees within federal offices or inspectors general are vested with law enforcement authority. For the purposes of this report, law enforcement authority is generally defined as having the legal authority to

- carry a firearm while engaged in official duties;[1]
- make an arrest without a warrant while engaged in official duties; and
- seek and execute warrants for arrest, search of premises, or seizure of evidence.[2]

According to some OIGs vested with law enforcement authority, these authorities are essential to certain missions of the office. In some cases, for example, OIG law enforcement officers conduct investigations that pose potential safety risks.

This report provides a list of the statutes and regulations that are used to vest OIGs with law enforcement authority. It also provides resources that add context to what some OIGs say is a need for law enforcement authority in their offices.

## WHY PURCHASE WEAPONS AND AMMUNITION?

Each federal agency, including OIGs, has a unique mission, and, therefore, a unique purpose for its law enforcement authority. In some cases, especially when Congress and the public demonstrate concern about the agency's weapons procurement, an agency may release a public statement detailing its law enforcement authority and its need to acquire weapons or ammunition.

For example, in August 2012, the Social Security Administration's (SSA's) OIG posted information on its blog explaining an ammunition purchase that garnered public attention. According to an excerpt from the post,

> Media reports expressed concerns over the type of ammunition ordered. In fact, this type of ammunition is standard issue for many law enforcement agencies. OIG's special agents use this ammunition during their mandatory quarterly firearms qualifications and other training sessions, to ensure agent and public safety. Additionally, the ammunition our agents use is the same type used at the Federal Law Enforcement Training Center.[3]

In another, more recent example, the U.S. Department of Agriculture's (USDA's) OIG received inquiries about OIG solicitations for weapons and body armor. The procurement pertained to the OIG's effort to replace automatic firearms with new semi-automatic firearms.[4] On May 19, 2014, Mr. Paul Feeney, deputy counsel at the OIG, sent the following response to questions about the procurement:

> The Inspector General Act of 1978 authorized OIG to, among other duties, pursue criminal activity, fraud, and abuses impairing USDA's program and operations. The criminal investigation responsibilities and impact of OIG are quite extensive—from fiscal year 2012 through March 2014, OIG investigations pertaining to USDA operations have obtained over 2,000 indictments, 1,350 convictions, and over $460 million in monetary results. OIG Special Agents are authorized to make arrests, execute warrants, and carry firearms.
>
> Regarding the need for weapons' procurements, and for defensive vests, USDA OIG's Investigations division conducts hundreds of criminal investigations each year, some of which involve OIG agents, USDA employees, and/or members of the public facing potentially life threatening situations. OIG special agents regularly conduct undercover operations and surveillance. The types of investigations conducted by

OIG special agents include criminal activities such as fraud in farm programs; significant thefts of Government property or funds; bribery and extortion; smuggling; and assaults and threats of violence against USDA employees engaged in their official duties.[5]

# SOURCES THAT VEST OIGS WITH LAW ENFORCEMENT AUTHORITY

Generally, there are three ways that an OIG can be vested with law enforcement authority.

- First, and most commonly, an OIG can be vested with law enforcement explicitly pursuant to Section 6(e)(3) of the IG Act of 1978, as amended (5 U.S.C. (IG Act) Appendix, Section 6(e)(4); hereinafter referred to as the IG Act).
- Second, an OIG can be vested with law enforcement authority by the Attorney General pursuant to criteria articulated in several provisions of Section 6(e) of the IG Act of 1978.
- Third, an OIG can be vested with law enforcement authority pursuant to statute outside of the IG Act of 1978, as is the case with six federal entities described below.

# THE INSPECTOR GENERAL ACT OF 1978

## Explicit Statutory Authority

As shown in *Table 1*, the IG Act provides direct law enforcement authority to 25 federal entities explicitly named in Section 6(e)(3) of the act.

## Authority Delegated by the Attorney General

As noted earlier, pursuant to Section 6 of the IG Act, the Attorney General is authorized to delegate law enforcement authority when

1. an OIG "is significantly hampered in the performance of responsibilities ... as a result of the lack of such powers";
2. "assistance from other law enforcement agencies is insufficient to meet the need for such powers"; and
3. "adequate internal safeguards and management procedures exist to ensure proper exercise of such powers" (5 U.S.C. (IG Act) Appendix, Section 6(e)(2)).[6]

**Table 1. Federal Offices of Inspectors General Vested with Law Enforcement**

| | |
|---|---|
| Department of Commerce | Federal Deposition Insurance Corporation |
| Department of Education | Federal Emergency Management Agency[a] |
| Department of Energy | General Services Administration |
| Department of Health and Human Services | National Aeronautics and Space Administration |
| Department of Homeland Security | Nuclear Regulatory Commission |
| Department of Housing and Urban Development | Office of Personnel Management |
| Department of the Interior | Railroad Retirement Board |
| Department of Justice | Small Business Administration |
| Department of Labor | Social Security Administration |
| Department of State | Tennessee Valley Authority |
| Department of Transportation | Agency for International Development |
| Department of the Treasury | Environmental Protection Agency |
| Department of Veterans Affairs | |

Source: 5 U.S.C. (IG Act) Appendix, §6(e)(3).

[a] The Federal Emergency Management Agency (FEMA) is a component agency of the Department of Homeland Security (DHS), and, therefore, the DHS IG oversees this component agency as well as other component agencies. FEMA does not have its own OIG. Therefore, although 25 federal entities are explicitly vested with law enforcement authority in the IG Act, in practice, 24 OIGs are vested with law enforcement authority.

The Attorney General has vested the OIGs within the 10 agencies listed below with law enforcement authority.

- The National Archives and Records Administration
- Amtrak
- The Peace Corps

- The Board of Governors of the Federal Reserve and Consumer Financial Protection Bureau
- The Corporation for National and Community Service
- The Export-Import Bank of the United States
- The National Science Foundation
- The Federal Housing Finance Agency
- The Securities and Exchange Commission
- Special Inspector General for Afghanistan Reconstruction.[7]

## Law Enforcement Responsibilities and Requirements Pursuant to the IG Act

The IG Act authorizes the Attorney General to promulgate guidelines "that govern the use of law enforcement powers" for these OIGs.[8] On December 8, 2003, then-Attorney General John Ashcroft promulgated such guidelines, providing OIGs further detail on their law enforcement authorities' scope and limitations.

Within these guidelines, Mr. Ashcroft wrote that employees within the OIGs who qualify for law enforcement authority are required to complete various training, including the Basic Criminal Investigator Training Program (or equivalent) and initial and "refresher firearms training and qualification."[9] OIGs are also required to heed the Department of Justice's (DOJ's) deadly force policy.[10]

According to Mr. Ashcroft's guidelines, OIGs vested with law enforcement authority through the IG Act must provide "periodic refresher" training in trial processes; federal criminal and civil legal updates; interviewing techniques and policy; law of arrest, search, and seizure; and physical conditioning and defensive tactics.[11] Additionally, the OIGs are responsible for following other DOJ law enforcement related policies and guidelines, must consult with DOJ before using electronic surveillance, and must receive other approval before beginning an undercover investigation.[12]

# OTHER OIGS WITH LAW ENFORCEMENT AUTHORITY

## Statutes That Vest Law Enforcement Authority

As shown in *Table 2*, five additional OIGs are provided law enforcement authority through laws outside of the IG Act.

**Table 2. Department and Agency OIGs with Law Enforcement Authority Provided by Statutes Outside of the IG Act of 1978, as Amended**

| Agency | Statutory Law Enforcement Authority |
|---|---|
| Department of Agriculture | Agriculture and Food Act of 1981; P.L. 97-98, Sec. 1337;<br>95 Stat. 1294; 7 U.S.C. §2270. |
| Department of Defense | Some law enforcement authority is provided by the National Defense Authorization Act of 1998; P.L. 105-85, Sec. 1071; 111 Stat. 1897; 10 U.S.C. §1585a; with authority to carry firearms delegated from the Secretary pursuant to 10 U.S.C. §1585. |
| U.S. Postal Service | Omnibus Consolidated Appropriations Act, 1997; P.L. 104-208. Sec. 207; 110 Stat. 3009-379; 39 U.S.C. §2009 note. |
| Treasury Inspector General for Tax Administration | Internal Revenue Service Restructuring and Reform Act of 1998; P.L. 105-206, Sec. 1103; 112 Stat. 707; 5 U.S.C. Appendix, §8D. |
| Special Inspector General for the Troubled Asset Relief Program | Special Inspector General for the Troubled Asset Relief Program Act of 2009; P.L. 111-15; 12 U.S.C. §5231(d)(3). |

# INSPECTOR GENERAL LAW ENFORCEMENT STAFF STATISTICS

The Department of Justice's Bureau of Justice Statistics maintains a *Census on Federal Law Enforcement Officers*, which includes data on the number of federal employees who are authorized to carry firearms.[13] The most recent report available states that 33 OIGs had a total of 3,501 agents who were authorized to carry firearms in September 2008.[14] Additionally, the report states that no law enforcement officers within an OIG were assaulted or injured in 2008.[15]

## End Notes

[1] Offices of inspectors general are "independent and objective units" within federal departments or agencies. Law enforcement authority permits certain OIG employees to carry firearms, among other authorities. Generally, an agency contracting office—not the OIG—purchases the goods and services an OIG needs to perform its mission, such as weapons, ammunition, and other law enforcement-related equipment and supplies. The Special Inspector General for Afghanistan Reconstruction, however, is provided explicit statutory contracting authority in its authorizing legislation (P.L. 110-181; National Defense Authorization Act for Fiscal Year 2008).

[2] Component agencies within a larger federal department or entity may be vested with statutory law enforcement authorities. The law enforcement authorities of federal agencies other than OIGs are beyond the scope of this report.

[3] Social Security Administration Office of Inspector General, "Social Security's OIG Responds to Concerns Over Ammunition Procurement," at http://oig.ssa.gov/newsroom/blog/2012/08/ social-securitys-oig-responds-concerns-overammunition-procurement.

[4] Pursuant to the Gun Control Act (GCA) of 1968, the term "semiautomatic rifle" is defined as any repeating rifle which utilizes a portion of the energy of a firing cartridge to extract the fired cartridge case and chamber the next round, and which requires a separate pull of the trigger to fire each cartridge (18 U.S.C. §921(a)(28)). "Semiautomatic pistol" and "rifle" are similarly defined in the Code of Federal Regulations (27 C.F.R. §478.11).

By comparison, pursuant to the 1934 National Firearms Act (NFA), the term "machine gun" is defined as any weapon which shoots, is designed to shoot, or can be readily restored to shoot, automatically more than one shot, without manual reloading, by a single function of the trigger. The term also includes the frame or receiver of any such weapon, any part designed and intended solely and exclusively, or combination of parts designed and intended, for use in converting a weapon into a machine gun, and any combination of parts from which a machinegun can be assembled if such parts are in the possession or under the control of a person (26 U.S.C. §5845(b)). Enacted as part of the Internal Revenue Code, the NFA levies taxes on all aspects of the manufacture/importation and distribution of such firearms, and requires that these firearms and their owners be registered at every point the firearms change ownership in the chain of commerce.

[5] Information provided to the author by USDA's OIG on May 19, 2014.

[6] Federal law and regulation (28 U.S.C. §566(c), 28 U.S.C. §561, and 28 C.F.R. §0.112) authorize the U.S. Marshals Service to deputize certain federal employees—which in some cases include OIG employees—with the ability to use existing law enforcement authorities across state boundaries to pursue particular investigations. See also U.S. Marshals Service, "17.11 Special Deputation Program, Tactical Operations Division (TOD)." According to the U.S. Marshals Service, certain employees within the OIGs of the following agencies are currently deputized by the Marshals Service: Amtrak, the Government Printing Office, the Library of Congress, the National Science Foundation, the Office of Personnel Management, the Smithsonian Institution, and the Social Security Administration. Additionally, Department of Labor OIG employees currently involved in a joint task force

under the direction of the Federal Bureau of Investigation have Marshals Service deputation. Information provided to the author from the U.S. Marshal Service via email on July 24, 2014.

[7] Information provided from the Department of Justice to the author via email on September 8, 2014.

[8] 5 U.S.C. (IG Act) Appendix, §6(e)(4)

[9] Office of the Attorney General, "Attorney General Guidelines for Offices of Inspector General with Statutory Law Enforcement Authority," p. 2, at https://www.ignet.gov/pande/standards/agleguidelines.pdf. Training is required to take place at the Federal Law Enforcement Training Center.

[10] U.S. Department of Justice, "Policy Statement: Use of Deadly Force," at http://www.justice.gov/ag/readingroom/ resolution14b.htm.

[11] Office of the Attorney General, "Attorney General Guidelines for Offices of Inspector General with Statutory Law Enforcement Authority," p. 2, at https://www.ignet.gov/pande/standards/agleguidelines.pdf.

[12] Ibid. For additional information on the requirements associated with an OIG's receipt of law enforcement authority, see Glenn A. Fine, "The New Statutory Law Enforcement Authority for OIG Criminal Investigators," The Journal of Public Inquiry, Spring/Summer 2003, pp. 15-22, at http://www.ignet.gov/randp/sp03jpi.pdf.

[13] U.S. Department of Justice, "Federal Law Enforcement Officers, 2008," June 2012, at http://www.bjs.gov/content/ pub/pdf/fleo08.pdf.

[14] Ibid., p. 6.

[15] Ibid., p. 9.

In: Federal Inspectors General
Editor: Emmett Cruz

ISBN: 978-1-63485-524-2


*Chapter 3*

# OVERSIGHT OF THE INSPECTOR GENERAL COMMUNITY: THE IG COUNCIL'S INTEGRITY COMMITTEE[*]

*Wendy Ginsberg*

## SUMMARY

The federal government has more than 70 federal inspectors general (IGs) who are vested with authority to combat waste, fraud, and abuse in their affiliated departments and agencies. This community of IGs serves a key role in assisting congressional oversight by conducting audits, investigations, and evaluations of their affiliated agencies, and by providing written reports at least two times a year to Congress.

The Inspector General Act of 1978 (5 U.S.C. Appendix), as amended, establishes an Integrity Committee (IC) that serves to oversee the appropriate conduct of high-ranking employees in the inspector general community and investigate allegations of wrongdoing against those employees. Ethical, transparent, and professional conduct is essential for members of the IG community because, as one Member of Congress stated at a February 2015 House Oversight and Government Reform hearing, "Your whole investigation is tainted if you're tainted."

---

[*] This is an edited, reformatted and augmented version of a Congressional Research Service, Publication No. R44198, dated September 21, 2015.

A few recent high-profile IC misconduct investigations have prompted concern from certain Members of Congress and the public. In one case, the length of an investigation allowed a federal IG to remain on paid administrative leave for more than two years. That IG eventually left his post before the results of the IC's investigation were made public.

Congress may also have concerns about a committee of IGs investigating allegations of wrongdoing made against their peers.

In the 114th Congress, both the House and the Senate are considering legislation to amend the operations of the IC. The bills, S. 579 and H.R. 2395, have some similar provisions including language seeking to limit the amount of time the IC would have to conduct investigations into allegations of IG employee wrongdoing—among other provisions.

Congress may determine that the IC's current structure is effective in ensuring the professional conduct of the IG community. Alternatively, Congress may determine that the IC is not the appropriate mechanism for IG community misconduct investigations. Instead, Congress may determine that another investigatory organization, like the Government Accountability Office, is better suited to oversee IG community conduct.

This report provides context on the role of the IC in investigating allegations of wrongdoing made against employees of the IG community. The report provides analysis of congressional proposals seeking to amend and improve the IC's operations, and includes additional potential policy options for improvement of oversight of the IG community.

## INTRODUCTION

Congress vested federal inspectors general (IGs) with the authority to combat waste, fraud, and abuse within designated federal departments and agencies. Offices of inspectors general (OIGs) exist in more than 70 federal agencies, including all departments and larger agencies, numerous boards and commissions, and other entities.[1]

The overwhelming majority of IGs are governed by the Inspector General Act of 1978, as amended (hereinafter referred to as the IG Act).[2] The IG Act provides various authorities—including hiring authorities and subpoena power—that give IGs autonomy to conduct thorough investigations and assessments of agency operations. The IG Act also establishes an Integrity Committee (IC) that serves to oversee the appropriate conduct of high-ranking employees in the inspector general community and investigate allegations of wrongdoing against those employees. As Representative Gerald Connolly stated at a February 3, 2015 hearing on IG independence, access, and authority, "Your whole investigation is tainted if you're tainted."[3] The IC can refer certain allegations of wrongdoing to authorities that would be the most appropriate venue for investigation—for example the Office of Special Counsel[4] or the Department of Justice. If the IC determines the IG community is the best venue to investigate certain allegations of wrongdoing, it may task a federal IG with conducting the investigation on the IC's behalf.

In the 114th Congress, both the House and the Senate are considering legislation to amend the operations of the IC. On February 26, 2015, Senate Homeland Security and Governmental Affairs Chairman Charles Grassley introduced the Inspector General Empowerment Act of 2015 (S. 579). On May 18, 2015, House Oversight and Government Reform Committee Chairman Jason Chaffetz introduced a companion to the Senate bill (H.R. 2395). Both bills seek to limit the amount of time the IC would have to conduct investigations into allegations of IG employee wrongdoing.

Congress, watchdog organizations, and the public have expressed concerns over the length of IC investigations, the structure of the IC's leadership, and the lack of congressional and public access to the results of IC investigations.

Congress has a variety of policy options that it may pursue if it chooses to amend the operations of CIGIE. For example, Congress could give the Government Accountability Office (GAO) a larger role in the investigation of allegations of wrongdoing made against members of the IG community—removing IGs from the role of overseeing themselves. Congress could also choose to restructure the IC's leadership, removing the Federal Bureau of Investigation (FBI) from chairmanship of the committee. Such an amendment could alter what some have considered an unbalanced focus on criminal allegations of wrongdoing rather than ethical wrongdoing. To increase the transparency of the IC's operations, Congress may also choose to increase the committee's reporting requirements.

This report examines the structure and operations of the IC, and provides analysis of certain policy options that could improve the committee's operations.

## Integrity Committee Structure and Operations

The IC is one of eight committees of the Council of the Inspectors General on Integrity and Efficiency (CIGIE), an interagency council in the executive branch that seeks to address issues of "integrity, economy, and effectiveness" that transcend individual agency jurisdictions.[5] Additionally, CIGIE seeks to develop "policies, standards, and approaches" that increase the "professionalism and effectiveness" of the IG workforce.[6] Members of the council include all federal IGs, among a few others: the FBI's appointed CIGIE member, the Deputy Director of the Office of Management and Budget (OMB), the Office of Federal Financial Management Controller (within OMB), the Director of the Office of Government Ethics, the Deputy Director for the Office of Personnel Management (OPM), and the Special Counsel. [7]

While CIGIE operates seven committees, only the IC is explicitly required by the IG Act. Pursuant to statute, the Integrity Committee "shall receive, review, and refer for investigation allegations of wrongdoing that are made against Inspectors General and staff members of the various" OIGs. [8] The Integrity Committee operates using funding collected from council members. The IG Act provides the Integrity Committee chairperson the authority to request resources from CIGIE members as well as request that member OIGs detail employees to assist any investigations.

The statute appoints the FBI's CIGIE member as the chairperson of the Integrity Committee.[9] The law requires the chief of the Public Integrity Section of the Criminal Division of DOJ, or his or her designee, to serve as the Integrity Committee's legal advisor.

The size, scope, and structure of CIGIE have come under public and congressional scrutiny recently,[10] focusing particular attention on the time that certain investigations have taken to complete and the opaque nature of the investigative process.[11] Additionally, the Integrity Committee has been criticized for not making public the results of investigations that find wrongdoing and not providing specific disciplinary recommendations for IG employees found to have committed wrongdoing.[12] In particular, S. 579, introduced by Senate Homeland Security and Governmental Affairs Committee Chairman Grassley, seeks to strengthen "the IC investigation process without being overly prescriptive."[13] Below the IC's processes and operations are examined to provide context for potential policy options to address some expressed concerns.

## Integrity Committee Process

Pursuant to law, IGs are required to refer to the Integrity Committee "any allegation of wrongdoing against a staff member" within his or her office under particular circumstances.[14] For example, referral is to occur if review of the allegation cannot be assigned to any other executive branch agency "with appropriate jurisdiction over the matter" and the IG determines "an objective internal investigation of the allegation" is not possible or might not appear objective.[15]

As shown in **Figure 1**, the Integrity Committee is required to review any received allegations of wrongdoing and refer them to the executive branch agency with appropriate jurisdiction.[16] In cases where an appropriate executive branch agency is unavailable, the allegation is referred to the Integrity Committee. In cases referred to the Integrity Committee, investigations into alleged wrongdoing are required to be "thorough and timely" and conducted pursuant to the most current standards.[17]

The IG Act provides the Integrity Committee the authority to establish additional policies and procedures to increase "fairness and consistency" in initiating, conducting, and reporting the results of an investigation.[18] These policies are to be reported to the congressional committees of jurisdiction.[19]

The chairperson of the Integrity Committee is required by statute to report the results of any of its investigations to the full committee.[20] Likewise, any executive branch agency tasked with investigating allegations of OIG employee wrongdoing must report its results to the Integrity Committee.[21] The committee is also required by statute to create policies and procedures that provide those accused of wrongdoing "an opportunity to respond to" any Integrity Committee report.[22]

The full Integrity Committee is then required within 30 days to forward the completed investigation to the CIGIE executive chairperson—complete with any recommended disciplinary actions.[23] In the case of allegations of wrongdoing against an employee at an establishment OIG (an OIG with an IG appointed by the President with the advice and consent of the Senate), the investigation report is to be provided to the President within 30 days of its completion. For allegations against an employee at a designated federal entity OIG (an OIG with an IG appointed by the applicable agency head), the report would be provided to the affiliated agency head within 30 days.[24] Within 30 days of providing the report with recommendations to CIGIE's executive chairperson, the Integrity Committee is required to provide to ap[25]licable congressional committees an "executive summary" of the investigation report. CIGIE's executive chairperson is required by statute to notify the Integrity Committee of any actions taken by the President, the agency head, or other entity, to resolve any matter relating to the investigation.[26]

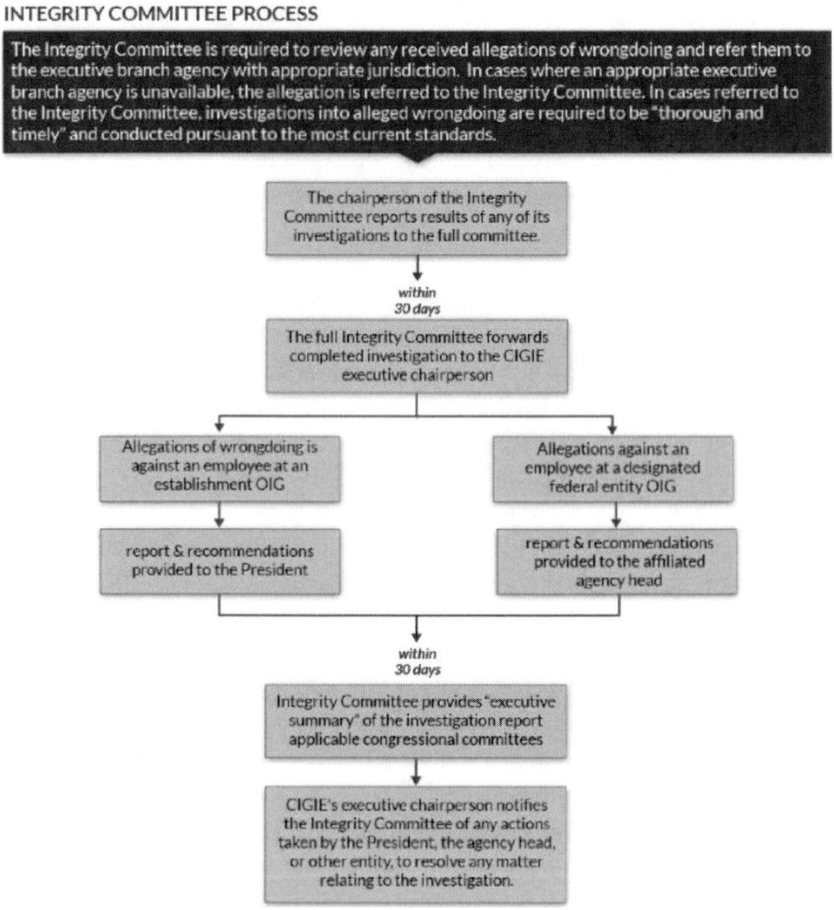


Source: Created by the Congressional Research Service based on statutory language found in 5 U.S.C. (IG Act) Appendix, §11(d).

Note: CIGIE is the Council of the Inspectors General on Integrity and Efficiency. OIG is Office of Inspector General.

Figure 1. The Integrity Committee's Investigatory Process.

As shown in **Figure 2**, pursuant to the IG Act, the Integrity Committee must report annually to Congress and the President on a number of items including

- the number of allegations of wrongdoing it received;
- the number of allegations of wrongdoing referred to other agencies, including criminal allegations;

- the number of allegations of wrongdoing closed without referral;
- dates of receipt and disposition of all allegations of wrongdoing; and
- the status of all investigations conducted by the Integrity Committee into allegations of wrongdoing, including the findings of completed investigations.[27]

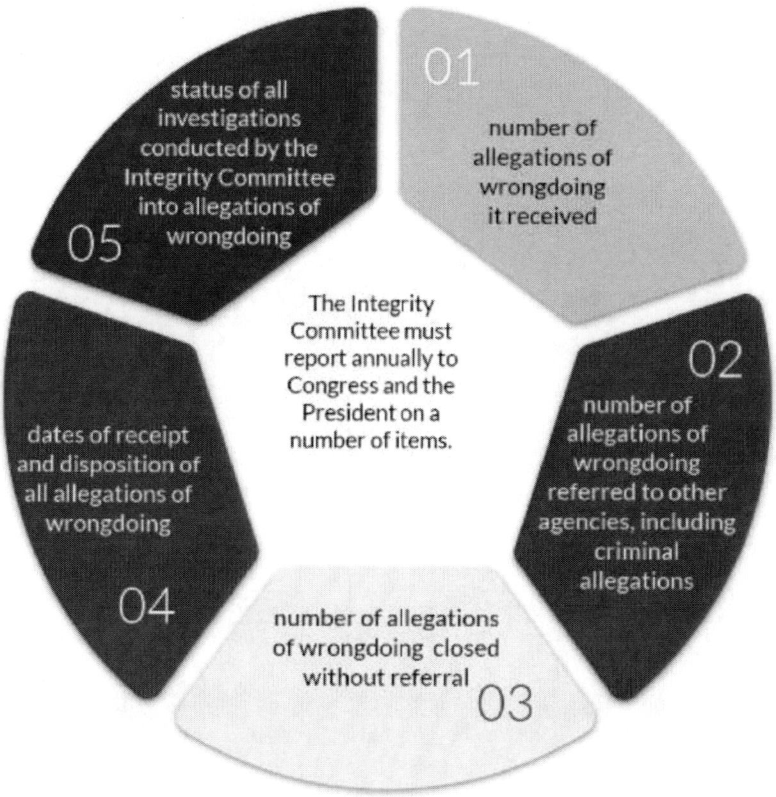


Source: Created by the Congressional Research Service based on the statutory language found in 5 U.S.C. (IG Act) Appendix, §11(d)(9).

Notes: The statute also provides for the chairperson or ranking Member of the House Committee on Oversight and Government Reform, the Senate Committee on Homeland Security and Governmental Affairs, and any applicable committee of jurisdiction to request additional information from CIGIE related to specific allegations.

Figure 2. The Contents of CIGIE's Annual Report to Congress.

## Allegations Received

In FY2014, the Integrity Committee reported receiving 72 allegations of wrongdoing, 37 of which were determined to be "outside" of the purview of CIGIE or the IG community.[28] Of the remaining 35 allegations of wrongdoing, 30 were reviewed and closed, four were referred for further investigation, and one allegation was "pending."[29] **Table 1** provides historical data on the number of allegations the Integrity Committee received, as well as data on allegations within the IC purview and the number of allegations that were referred for investigation.

**Table 1. Integrity Committee Annual Investigative Workload FY2009-FY20 14**

| Fiscal Year | Allegations Received | Allegations Within IC Purview | Allegations Closed | Allegations Referred to Committee Chair for Investigation | Allegations Referred to Appropriate Agency | Allegations Pending Review |
|---|---|---|---|---|---|---|
| 2009 | 43 | 38 | 36 | 2 | 5 | 0 |
| 2010 | 44 | 43 | 36 | 1 | 1 | 6 |
| 2011 | 51 | 28 | 22 | 1 | 23 | 5 |
| 2012 | 44 | 19 | 8 | 3 | 25 | 8 |
| 2013 | 390[a] | 374[a] | 361[a] | 12 | 16 | 1 |
| 2014 | 72 | 35 | 30 | 4 | 37 | 1 |

Source: CIGIE Annual Reports, available at https://www.ignet.gov/content/reports-publications.

[a] According to CIGIE, of the allegations received in FY2013, 312 concerned allegations previously reviewed and closed. No other information was available on the increase of allegations in this year. See Council of the Inspectors General on Integrity and Efficiency, *Progress Report to the President: Fiscal Year 2013*, Washington, DC, p. 5, at https://www.ignet.gov/sites/default/files/files/CIGIE%202013%20Progess%20Report.pdf.

# Concerns with the Integrity Committee's Operations

Some Members of Congress and the public have expressed concerns about the operations of the Integrity Committee, focusing particular attention on the lengths of time that certain investigations have taken and the opaque nature of the investigative process.[30] Additionally, the Integrity Committee has been criticized for not making public the results of investigations that find wrongdoing and for not providing the President, agency heads, or Congress specific recommendations for holding accountable IG employees found to have committed wrongdoing.[31]

**Case Study: The Integrity Committee Investigation of the National Archives and Records Administration Inspector General**

Beginning in June 2012, CIGIE received "numerous" allegations about a variety of inappropriate behavior by the National Archives and Records Administration (NARA) IG, counsel to the IG, and the assistant IG for investigations.[32] According to CIGIE, allegations of wrongdoing included

- "various statements the IG may have made concerning the race and/or ethnicity" of NARA employees;
- "comments about dating NARA employees" or contractors;
- comments "sexual in nature" about employees or contractors;
- "comments about the weight or personal appearance of employees" or contractors;
- "threatening comments about the NARA General Counsel"; and
- "a failure to follow appropriate investigative and audit standards and taking retaliatory actions against OIG employees."[33]

In July 2013, the Federal Deposit Insurance Corporation OIG (FDIC OIG) accepted the Integrity Committee's request to conduct an investigation into the allegations against the NARA OIG employees.[34] In May 2014, the FDIC OIG provided its findings to the Integrity Committee, which substantiated the allegations of various inappropriate comments made by the NARA IG. The FDIC OIG report stated it was "not able to substantiate the allegation" of failure to follow appropriate investigative and audit standards.

Throughout the entirety of the FDIC OIG investigation, the NARA IG was placed on paid administrative leave.

On May 21, 2014, the Integrity Committee met to discuss the FDIC OIG's findings. The IC "accepted and adopted" the investigation's findings and concluded that the NARA IG's behaviors "constituted administrative misconduct and undermined the integrity reasonably expected of an IG."[35] Neither the counsel to the IG nor the assistant IG for investigations was found to have "committed administrative misconduct."

From the time the IC received allegations of wrongdoing against NARA OIG officials to completion of the investigation, more than two years elapsed. In fact, the NARA OIG reportedly resigned from office in August 2014 when a copy of the FDIC OIG investigation's findings were leaked to the *Washington Post*.[36] It is unclear whether the agency head or Congress had been provided the FDIC OIG findings or the Integrity Committee's recommendations prior to the report's leak to the *Washington Post*.

Throughout the investigation process, several lawmakers criticized the length of time it was taking to complete. For example, on February 21, 2014, Representative Darrell Issa, Senator Charles E. Grassley, and then-Senator Tom A. Coburn wrote a joint letter to the Archivist expressing concern over the "use of extended, paid administrative leave" for the NARA IG, as well as whether the IG Act "adequately ensures that Congress receives formal notice and explanation when an agency takes action to prevent an IG from performing his duties."[37] On August 21, 2014, Senator Grassley wrote to the IC chairman expressing concerns about "[e]xtended investigations" that "are harmful to the independence and integrity of the IG community." Senator Grassley also noted that placing an IG on administrative leave for extended periods of time could constitute de facto removal of an IG from his or her office.[38]

In his February 3, 2015, testimony before the House Committee on Oversight and Government Reform, CIGIE's Chairman, Michael E. Horowitz, the IG at DOJ, stated,

> I am aware of the recent questions that have been raised relating to the work of CIGIE's Integrity Committee, including with respect to the timeliness of its work and the transparency of its efforts. One of my first meetings as Chair of CIGIE was with the Assistant Director of the FBI, who chairs the Integrity Committee, in order to discuss ways to address these issues. OIGs must maintain the highest levels of accountability and integrity, and as Chair of CIGIE I will make it a top priority to improve the procedures for the Integrity Committee.[39]

Certain Members of Congress and a watchdog organization have also expressed concerns with the reporting requirements of the IC and the IC's role in recommending actions, including disciplinary action, to be taken after completion of an investigation. For example, the IC is not required to provide the final report of its investigations into allegations of wrongdoing to Congress. Instead, as noted above, Congress receives an "executive summary" of the investigation.[40] Additionally, the Project on Government Oversight, an independent watchdog organization, has requested that the IC offer more precise recommendations for sanctions against or removal of IGs found to have committed wrongdoing.[41]

## RECENT LEGISLATION TO AMEND THE INTEGRITY COMMITTEE'S STRUCTURE AND OPERATIONS

In the 114[th] Congress, companion bills have been introduced that would amend the structure and operations of the IC. In the Senate, S. 579, introduced by Senate Homeland Security and Governmental Affairs Committee Chairman Grassley, seeks to strengthen "the IC investigation process without being overly prescriptive."[42] A similar bill, H.R. 2395, was introduced by House Oversight and Government Reform Committee Chairman Chaffetz. Provisions from each bill, as reported, are provided below as well as in an abbreviated form in **Table 2**.

### Time Limits on Investigations (S. 579 and H.R. 2395)

Both S. 579 and H.R. 2395 would place time limits on the completion of Integrity Committee investigations. Pursuant to S. 579, within seven days of the Integrity Committee's receipt of an allegation of wrongdoing against an IG or qualifying OIG staff, the allegation would be required to be appropriately referred to either the DOJ, the Office of Special Counsel, or the Integrity Committee—presumably dependent upon the substance of the allegation. If such an allegation were submitted to the Integrity Committee, S. 579 would provide the committee up to an additional seven days to determine whether the allegations warrant initiation of an investigation. The bill seeks to require that OIGs assigned to investigate allegations of wrongdoing by another IG or IG staff member are of "similar size." S. 579 would require completion of the investigation within 120 days of the Integrity Committee's referral for investigation. If the investigation could not be completed within 120 days, S. 579 would require the investigating IG to "notify" and "brief" the appropriate congressional committees of jurisdiction[43] every 30 days until the investigation was completed. The Senate report to accompany S. 579 stated that the provision "puts time limits on each significant step in the investigation to ensure the IC is moving efficiently toward completing the investigation and keeping Congress apprised of delays as well as informed of the results."[44]

H.R. 2395, by comparison, seeks to amend the IC's process by providing up to 60 days for the Integrity Committee to determine whether to initiate an investigation into an allegation of wrongdoing and then capping any investigation undertaken by the committee at six months. Pursuant to the provisions, if the investigation takes longer than the six-month cap, the committee would notify certain congressional committees of the need for an extension, and "to the maximum extent practicable, complete the investigation" within an additional three months. If the investigation lasts longer than nine months, the committee would be required to "brief" certain congressional committees every 30 days until the investigation was completed.

## Concurrent Investigation (S. 579 and H.R. 2395)

S. 579 and H.R. 2395 would permit the Integrity Committee to conduct any investigation even if their investigation ran concurrently with another oversight entity's investigation into the same allegation. For example, the Integrity Committee could investigate an allegation of wrongdoing for ethics, fraud, or other improprieties, while at the same time DOJ was investigating the allegation for criminal violations. Until a recent administrative chance in policy, if an allegation was referred to DOJ for investigation into potential criminal infractions, the Integrity Committee ceased any ongoing non-criminal investigation into that allegation. At a January 2015 meeting, CIGIE officials stated that in many cases, FBI investigations into allegations of IG wrongdoing prompted lengthy Integrity Committee investigation.[45] Earlier this year, however, the IC administratively determined that it may now conduct concurrent investigations. Congress, however, may decide that allowing concurrent investigation should be codified in statute. In other cases, Congress has stated that unclear or overlapping jurisdiction between the Integrity Committee and the Office of Special Council have hindered or delayed investigations into allegations of IG community wrongdoing.[46]

## Restructuring the Integrity Committee (S. 579)

S. 579 would amend the IG Act by removing the Special Counsel of the Office of Special Counsel from Integrity Committee membership, and removing the FBI official's statutory designation as the IC's chairperson. Instead, S. 579 seeks to provide authority to Integrity Committee members to elect, for a two-year term, a chairperson from among the IGs who are members of CIGIE. These provisions seek to address concerns, according to the Senate Committee Report, that "the chairmanship of the IC is a largely administrative role that has not been embraced by FBI and is better served by another party."[47]

## Reporting Requirements (S. 579)

Pursuant to S. 579, the results of any investigation—whether conducted by the Integrity Committee, DOJ, or the Office of Special Counsel—would have to be submitted to the Integrity Committee chairperson. In addition, the bill would ensure that Members of Congress have access "to any report authored by the Integrity Committee," and would require that any investigation final report be submitted, with Integrity Committee recommendations, to the Senate Committee on Homeland Security and Governmental Affairs, the House Committee on Oversight and Government Reform, and other appropriate congressional committees of jurisdiction. These provisions seek to keep Congress "informed of the results" of IC investigations.[48]

## Increased Investigatory Jurisdiction (S. 579)

S. 579 seeks to provide the Integrity Committee the authority to investigate allegations of wrongdoing against the Special Counsel or Deputy Special Counsel. The bill provides the Integrity Committee the authority to promulgate "regulations necessary" to execute such investigations.

## Selecting an Appropriate Investigator (H.R. 2395)

H.R. 2395 would formalize the process the Integrity Committee currently uses to select an IG to investigate allegations of wrongdoing made against OIG employees. As noted above, the IC does not investigate the allegations itself; it delegates that responsibility to a particular IG. H.R. 2395 would require CIGIE to create "a regular rotation" of IGs that can be "assigned to investigate complaints." The provisions also require the IC to create procedures that ensure IC investigations "avoid conflicts of interest." This provision appears to codify procedures already performed by the IC.

**Table 2. Legislative Provisions Seeking to Add Time Caps on Integrity Committee Investigations S. 579 and H.R. 2395**

| Provisions | S. 579 | H.R. 2395 |
|---|---|---|
| Time for Committee to Determine whether to Refer a Case for Investigation | Seven days to determine whether the allegation should be referred to either DOJ or the Office of Special Counsel.<br>If the IC decides to further pursue the case itself, the bill would provide the committee an additional seven days to determine whether the allegations warrant initiation of an investigation. | Up to 60 days. |
| Time for IC Committee to Complete an Investigation | 120 days, starting at the point the investigation was referred to the committee.<br>If the investigation lasts longer than the 120-day cap, the investigating IG would be required to "notify" and "brief" applicable congressional committees every 30 days until the investigation's completion. | Six months.<br>If the investigation needs additional time to complete, the IC can notify applicable congressional committees and would receive an additional three months.<br>After expiration of a nine-month investigation period, members of the IC would be required to brief appropriate congressional committees on the investigation every 30 days until the investigation was completed. |

| Provisions | S. 579 | H.R. 2395 |
|---|---|---|
| Concurrent Investigation | Would permit concurrent investigations by the IC, Office of Special Counsel, DOJ, or other appropriate entities. | Would permit concurrent investigations by the IC, Office of Special Counsel, DOJ, or other appropriate entities. |
| Restructuring the Integrity Committee | Would amend the IG Act by removing the Special Counsel of the Office of Special Counsel from Integrity Committee membership, and removing the FBI official's statutory designation as the IC's chairperson.<br>Would allow for the election of a CIGIE member to serve as the IC's chairperson. | N/A |
| Reporting Requirements | Would require the submission of results of any investigation of an IG community employee—whether conducted by the Integrity Committee, DOJ, or the Office of Special Counsel—to the Integrity Committee chairperson.<br>Would ensure that Members of Congress have access "to any report authored by the Integrity Committee," | N/A |
| Increased Investigatory Jurisdiction | Would provide the IC authority to investigate allegations of wrongdoing against the Special Counsel or Deputy Special Counsel. | N/A |
| Selecting an Appropriate Investigator | N/A | Would formalize the process the IC uses to select an IG to investigate allegations of wrongdoing made against OIG employees by statutorily requiring the establishment of "a regular rotation" of IGs that can be "assigned to investigate complaints." |

Source: The text of S. 579 and H.R. 2395 is available in the Legislative Information System (LIS) at http://www.lis.gov/.

## Previous Congresses

The 114th Congress is not the first in which legislators introduced legislation to amend the operations of CIGIE and the Integrity Committee. H.R. 5492 (113th Congress) sought to amend CIGIE's statutory authority by placing time limits on the Integrity Committee's determination of whether to investigate allegations of wrongdoing against an IG and certain other IG employees. Like H.R. 2395 in the 114th Congress, H.R. 5492 also would have initially limited an Integrity Committee investigation to six months with a potential to gain an additional three months. To gain the additional three months, the Integrity Committee would be required to notify appropriate congressional committees of jurisdiction of the need for additional time. If the Integrity Committee determined that an investigation needed additional time beyond nine months, the Integrity Committee would be required to brief Members of the House Committee on Oversight and Government Reform, the Senate Committee on Homeland Security and Governmental Affairs, and other applicable committees of jurisdiction about the progress of the investigation every 30 days until the investigation's completion.

H.R. 5815 (111th Congress) contained provisions nearly identical to S. 579 (114th Congress) that sought to authorize the IC to investigate allegations of wrongdoing against the Special Counsel or Deputy Special Counsel.

# ANALYSIS

Both chambers of Congress have demonstrated an interest in amending the operations of the IC. The sections below examine in more detail the major concepts proposed in legislation in the 114th Congress.

## The Length of Integrity Committee Investigations

As noted in the sections above, these bills focus on the length of time the IC takes to investigate allegations of wrongdoing made against high-ranking IG community staff. For example, both bills would cap the length of time the Integrity Committee would have to refer an investigation to the appropriate authority. These bills also seek to cap the time an investigation can take, if the appropriate referral authority is the IC itself.

IGs strive to root out waste, fraud, and abuse in their affiliated agencies. Allegations of waste, fraud, or abuse within the OIG community can prompt doubt in IG findings or can cause inappropriate use of finite federal resources. As noted above, Members of Congress have emphasized the importance of expeditiously investigating allegations of misconduct by IGs and other high-ranking OIG officials. Yet, there is also concern to ensure that those accused of wrongdoing are provided the opportunity to demonstrate innocence, providing needed context to an investigation. CIGIE is in a unique position to oversee investigations into allegations of wrongdoing and keep applicable congressional committees of jurisdiction apprised of the investigation's progress. The substance of an IG investigation is sensitive—even the knowledge that someone is the subject of an ongoing investigation into alleged misconduct can negatively affect his or her career, regardless of the investigation's findings. The IC, therefore, may be concerned about sharing information on ongoing or even completed investigations with Congress or the public.

Congress, however, has an interest in ensuring that the IG community is appropriately overseen as well. The Integrity Committee is one tool Congress has to root out waste, fraud, or abuse in the IG community. Congress may choose to limit the time the IC has to complete an investigation, as S. 579 and H.R. 2395 seek to do.

Another mechanism Congress may choose to employ is requiring GAO to investigate an allegation of wrongdoing in lieu of the Integrity Committee. GAO has, historically, performed such reviews of allegations of misconduct waged against an OIG.[49] Replacing the IC with GAO would remove the responsibility of policing the IG community from CIGIE in the executive branch and place it with GAO in the legislative branch. GAO is not a member of CIGIE and would, therefore, remove any concerns with the IG community policing itself. GAO, however, may not have the capacity to investigate all allegations of wrongdoing in the IG community. GAO also may not be capable of investigating wrongdoing at IGs of a significantly larger size, like the Department of Defense or the Department of Health and Human Services OIG.

In lieu of assigning all investigatory responsibilities to GAO, Congress may choose to require GAO to select a sample of investigations into wrongdoing allegations conducted by IGs on behalf of the Integrity Committee and examine their efficacy. This policy option would establish an audit of IC investigations. If Congress chose this policy option, it would provide an additional check on the IG community's oversight of itself. This additional layer of oversight, however, could increase the length of time it would take to come to a final conclusion about a particular investigation.

## Concurrent Investigation

As noted above, until a recent administrative change by the IC, some IC investigations were suspended while DOJ or the Office of Special Counsel examined allegations that fell within their jurisdictions. DOJ, for example, would examine a case with potential criminal implications. The Office of Special Counsel may come into play when a federal agency uses prohibited personnel practices against an employee. When either of these federal agencies investigated allegations of wrongdoing made against a member of the IG community, any investigation of those allegations conducted on behalf of the IC previously ceased. The IC investigation could not resume until the other entities finished their investigations. Sometimes, as in the case of the investigation of the NARA IG, these stoppages lasted for long stretches of time. Although the IC has administratively eliminated the prohibition on concurrent investigation, Congress may decide to codify the authority to conduct concurrent investigation. Codifying the authority to conduct concurrent investigation could allow the IC to complete its investigations more quickly, thereby saving time, resources, and money over the longer term. Codification would also reinforce the IC's administrative decision to permit concurrent investigation, should any of the other investigatory bodies object to the IC's new policy. Concurrent investigation could, however, prompt investigative redundancy thereby adding to the shorter-term time and costs each investigating entity may have to incur.

## Integrity Committee Structure

The membership of the IC, particularly for leadership positions, has been of concern to Congress and the public since the IC's statutory establishment. As noted above, Congress has expressed reservations that the current leadership structure, which taps the FBI's CIGIE representative as the IC chairman, has not been as effective as desired. Additionally, the Project on Government Oversight (POGO), the independent watchdog organization, has expressed concerns that an FBI representative "may overlook misconduct or inappropriate behavior that does not actually violate any laws" because of the

FBI's focus on criminal violations.[50] Citing a former DOD OIG official as its source, POGO wrote, "criminal investigators should not be in charge of administrative inquiries."[51]

S. 579 includes provisions that would remove the FBI's CIGIE representative from the IC chairmanship and render the post an elected position, chosen for a two-year term from among CIGIE's membership. Such an amendment could improve the operations of the IC committee by placing a chairman at the committee's helm whose expertise more clearly align with the assignments and goals of the IC. Additionally, the amendment would establish the IC chairmanship post as the only statutorily established CIGIE position in which a special IG[52] or an IG affiliated with a legislative branch entity[53] were authorized to serve. Currently, only IGs established explicitly through the IG Act of 1978, as amended, are authorized to hold statutorily established CIGIE leadership roles. The language, therefore, could be seen to make CIGIE more inclusive of all its members. Accordingly, the FBI's CIGIE representative would still be eligible to serve in the post if elected.

On the other hand, electing an IG to the chairmanship of a committee charged with investigating wrongdoing of his or her colleagues may prompt concerns that the IC lacks the impartiality necessary to conduct such sensitive work. Removing a non-IG official from the chairmanship of the IC committee could prompt conflict-of-interest concerns that IGs—who often know and work with one another—may not be aggressive enough in their investigations of alleged wrongdoing.

Congress has a number of potential options regarding future leadership of the Integrity Committee. On the one hand, the existing leadership structure could remain unchanged, with the FBI's CIGIE representative continuing to serve as the IC's chairperson. Congress may choose, on the other hand, to enact the provisions of S. 579 that would make the chairperson's position an elected one. Congress might also consider requiring another of CIGIE's non-IG members to serve as chair, or even bring in new leadership from outside the council. For example, Congress could require the Special Counsel of the Office of Special Counsel, a CIGIE member, to serve as chairperson or share the leadership position with the FBI representative, thereby embedding both criminal and civil oversight expertise into the role. Additionally, Congress could choose to appoint the Director of the Office of Government Ethics, also a CIGIE member, as the IC chairman, refocusing the committee on ethical violations and allowing referral to DOJ for criminal infractions. Congress might also choose to appoint someone from outside of CIGIE's membership to the leadership structure of the IC. For example, Congress could appoint the

Comptroller General or another GAO representative to serve as the IC chairperson or in another IC leadership role. Placing a GAO representative at the helm of the committee could remove any perception of a conflict of interest while retaining knowledge of IG community operations and expectations.

## Additional Reporting Requirements

Congress needs access to accurate, authoritative, and timely materials to conduct effective oversight of IGs. Currently, the IC is required to provide appropriate committees of Congress an executive summary of any investigation conducted by the IC. Provisions in S. 579 would require that all investigations into IG employees—whether conducted by the Integrity Committee, DOJ, or the Office of Special Counsel—be provided to Congress. The provisions would also ensure that Congress receives the report of the full investigation, with recommendations—and not an executive summary of the investigation.

Access to the full investigation results could provide greater context to certain investigations and assist Congress in determining whether additional actions to discipline or remove an OIG employee need to be taken. The contents of investigations are sensitive. As noted above, even the knowledge that a particular IG or employee is under investigation could harm his or her career. Congress may determine that the current level of access to IC reports is an appropriate balance between protection of sensitive information and information access that allows for effective congressional oversight.

## Increased Investigatory Jurisdiction

S. 579 would increase the IC's investigatory jurisdiction to include authority to investigate allegations of wrongdoing against the Special Counsel and the Deputy Special Counsel. These positions have unique roles in the federal government, but possess a skill set that may be similar to that of an IG. The IC, therefore, may be an appropriate entity to lead an investigation into allegations of wrongdoing. Alternatively, the differences between a special counsel and an IG may render an IC investigation less useful than another entity's investigation.

The provision expanding the IC's jurisdiction would vest the IC with the authority to promulgate "regulations necessary" to perform these new duties. Among the items these regulations might need to address are the following:

- Which IGs could be tasked with performing an investigation?
- Would the Special Counsel have to recuse himself or herself from the IC during any ongoing investigation involving the Special Counsel or the Deputy?
- Which office would pay for any investigations involving the Office of Special Counsel?
- Could the IC make recommendations for remedial action against or removal of the Special Counsel or the Deputy Special Counsel?

## End Notes

[1] Three other inspector general posts (in the armed forces departments) are recognized in public law: Air Force (10 U.S.C. §8020), Army (10 U.S.C. §3020), and Navy (10 U.S.C. §5020). These offices, however, are not often included in tallies of federal inspectors general because they have a significantly different heritage, set of authorities, operational structure and organization, and degree of independence.

[2] 5 U.S.C. (IG Act) Appendix.

[3] U.S. Congress, House Committee on Oversight and Government Reform, *Inspectors General: Independence, Access and Authority*, 1st sess., February 3, 2015, at https://oversight.house.gov/hearing/inspectors-general-independenceaccess-authority-2/. Representative Connolly's statement is made around the 1:15:00 mark.

[4] The Office of Special Counsel is authorized to "safeguard the merit system by protecting federal employees and applicants from prohibited personnel practices, especially reprisal for whistleblowing." See Office of Special Counsel, "About," at https://osc.gov/pages/about.aspx.

[5] 5 U.S.C. (IG Act) Appendix, §11(d)(4)(A). Council of the Inspectors General for Integrity and Efficiency, "Mission and Organization," at http://www.ignet.gov/cigie1.html.

[6] Ibid.

[7] 5 U.S.C (IG Act), §11(d)(2).

[8] 5 U.S.C. (IG Act) Appendix, §11(d)(1). Staff members who can be investigated for wrongdoing pursuant to this provision include any OIG employee who reports directly to the IG and any staff member designated by the IG as a staff member in an annual submission to the Integrity Committee.

[9] 5 U.S.C. (IG Act) Appendix, §11(d)(2). The FBI's designee is not an IG.

[10] See, for example, Letter from Senator Charles E. Grassley, Ranking Member on the Committee on the Judiciary, to Joseph S. Campbell, Committee Chairman of the CIGIE Integrity Committee, August 21, 2014, http://www.grassley.senate.gov/sites/default/files/news/upload/CEG%20to%20CIGIE%20IC%20%28timelines%29%2C%208-21-14.pdf; and U.S. Congress, Senate Committee on Homeland Security and Governmental Affairs, *To*

*Amend the Inspector General Act of 1978 To Strengthen the Independence of the Inspectors General, and for Other Purposes*, report to accompany S. 579, 114th Cong., 1st sess., May 5, 2015, S.Rept. 114-36 (Washington: GPO, 2015).

[11] The Project on Government Oversight, a watchdog organization that works for government reforms, released a report in 2009 that found many in the IG community expressed concerns about a lack of transparency in the IC's operations. See, Project on Government Oversight, "Inspectors General: Accountability is a Balancing Act," p. 10, at http://www.pogoarchives.org/m/go/ig/accountability/ig-accountability-20090320.pdf.

[12] See Project on Government Oversight, "Inspectors General: Accountability is a Balancing Act," p. 11, at http://www.pogoarchives.org/m/go/ig/accountability/ig-accountability-20090320.pdf. As noted above, the IG Act requires the IC to provide recommendations on potential disciplinary action anyone found to have committed wrongdoing.

[13] U.S. Congress, Senate Committee on Homeland Security and Governmental Affairs, *To Amend the Inspector General Act of 1978 To Strengthen the Independence of the Inspectors General, and for Other Purposes*, report to accompany S. 579, 114th Cong., 1st sess., May 5, 2015, S.Rept. 114-36 (Washington: GPO, 2015), p. 12.

[14] The IC is authorized to examine and investigate allegations of wrongdoing made against an IG, anyone who "reports directly to an Inspector General, or any of the OIG staff the IG has designated for inclusion as part of an annual submission made to the CIGIE chairman. 5 U.S.C. (IG Act) Appendix, §11(d)(4).

[15] 5 U.S.C. (IG Act) Appendix, §11(d)(4).

[16] 5 U.S.C. (IG Act) Appendix, §11(d)(5).

[17] 5 U.S.C. (IG Act) Appendix, §11(d)(6).

[18] 5 U.S.C. (IG Act) Appendix, §11(d)(7)(B).

[19] 5 U.S.C. (IG Act) Appendix, §11(d)(7)(B)(ii).

[20] 5 U.S.C. (IG Act) Appendix, §11(d)(7)(C)(i).

[21] 5 U.S.C. (IG Act) Appendix, §11(d)(7)(C)(ii).

[22] 5 U.S.C. (IG Act) Appendix, §11(d)(7)(B)(i)(IV).

[23] 5 U.S.C. (IG Act) Appendix, §11(d)(8)(A).

[24] 5 U.S.C. (IG Act) Appendix, §11(d)(8)(A)(ii).

[25] 5 U.S.C. (IG Act) Appendix, §11(d)(8)(A)(iii).

[26] 5 U.S.C. (IG Act) Appendix, §11(d)(8)(B).

[27] 5 U.S.C. (IG Act) Appendix, §11(d)(9). The statute also provides for the chairperson or ranking Member of the House Committee on Oversight and Government Reform, the Senate Committee on Homeland Security and Governmental Affairs, and any applicable committee of jurisdiction to request additional information from CIGIE related to specific allegations.

[28] Council of the Inspectors General on Integrity and Efficiency: Integrity Committee, *Fiscal Year 2014 Annual Report to Congress and the President*, Washington, DC, December 15, 2014, at https://www.ignet.gov/sites/default/files/files/ FY%202014%20IC%20Annual%20 Report%20-%2012-22-14.pdf. When an allegation is found to be outside of the purview of the IC, it may be referred to another more appropriate entity for further investigation, such as the Department of Justice or the Office of Special Counsel.

[29] Ibid. Each allegation may not be unique. For example, in certain cases, multiple allegations can be made that could result in a single investigation.

[30] For one example of concern over the timeliness of an investigation that arose from a watchdog organization, see above "Case Study: The Integrity Committee Investigation of the National Archives and Records Administration Inspector General." The Project on Government

Oversight, a private organization that works for government reform, also released a report in 2009 that found many in the IG community expressed concerns about a lack of transparency in the IC's operations. See Project on Government Oversight, "Inspectors General: Accountability is a Balancing Act," p. 10, at http://www.pogoarchives.org/m/go/ig/accountability/ig-accountability-20090320.pdf.

31 See Project on Government Oversight, "Inspectors General: Accountability is a Balancing Act," p. 11, at http://www.pogoarchives.org/m/go/ig/accountability/ig-accountability-20090320.pdf. As noted above, the IG Act requires the IC to provide recommendations on potential disciplinary action of anyone found to have committed wrongdoing.

32 Council of the Inspectors General on Integrity and Efficiency: Integrity Committee, *Fiscal Year 2014 Annual Report to Congress and the President*, Washington, DC, December 15, 2014, at p. 3 of 6, https://www.ignet.gov/sites/default/ files/files/FY%202014%20IC%20Annual%20Report%20-%2012-22-14.pdf.

33 Ibid.

34 Ibid.

35 Ibid.

36 Lisa Rein, "Embattled National Archives IG to Retire After Probe Finds Misconduct," *Washington Post*, August 4, 2014, at http://www.washingtonpost.com/blogs/federal-eye/wp/2014/08/04/embattled-national-archives-ig-to-retireafter-probe-finds-misconduct/.

37 Letter from Senator Charles E. Grassley, Ranking Member of the Senate Committee on the Judiciary, Representative Darrell Issa, Chairman of the House Committee on Oversight and Government Reform, and Senator Tom A. Coburn, Ranking Member of the Senate Committee on Homeland Security and Governmental Affairs, to David Ferriero, Archivist of the United States, February 21, 2014. Letter provided to the author by staff from the Senate Committee on the Judiciary on February 23, 2015.

38 Letter from Senator Charles E. Grassley, Ranking Member on the Committee on the Judiciary, to Joseph S. Campbell, Committee Chairman of the CIGIE Integrity Committee, August 21, 2014, http://www.grassley.senate.gov/sites/default/files/news/upload/CEG%20to%20CIGIE%20IC%20%28timelines%29%2C%208-21-14.pdf.

39 U.S. Congress, House Committee on Oversight and Government Reform, *Inspectors General: Independence, Access and Authority*, testimony of CIGIE Chairman Michael E. Horowitz, 114th Cong., 1st sess., February 3, 2015, at http://oversight.house.gov/wp-content/uploads/2015/02/IG-Horowitz-CIGIE-Chair-Statement-2-3.pdf.

40 5 U.S.C. (IG Act) Appendix, §11(d).

41 Project on Government Oversight, *Inspectors General: Accountability is a Balancing Act*, 2009, March 20, 2009, pp. 10-11, at http://www.pogoarchives.org/m/go/ig/accountability/ig-accountability-20090320.pdf.

42 U.S. Congress, Senate Committee on Homeland Security and Governmental Affairs, *To Amend the Inspector General Act of 1978 To Strengthen the Independence of the Inspectors General, and for Other Purposes*, report to accompany S. 579, 114th Cong., 1st sess., May 5, 2015, S.Rept. 114-36 (Washington: GPO, 2015), p. 12.

43 These committees would include the House Committee on Oversight and Government Reform, the Senate Committee on Homeland Security and Governmental Affairs, and other applicable committees of substantive jurisdiction.

44 Ibid.

45 Information provided from CIGIE officials to the author at a January 29, 2015, meeting at the Congressional Research Service.

[46] U.S. Congress, Senate Committee on Homeland Security and Governmental Affairs, *To Amend the Inspector General Act of 1978 To Strengthen the Independence of the Inspectors General, and for Other Purposes*, report to accompany S. 579, 114th Cong., 1st sess., May 5, 2015, S.Rept. 114-36 (Washington: GPO, 2015), p. 11.

[47] Ibid., p. 12.

[48] Ibid.

[49] See, for example, U.S. General Accounting Office, *Financial Markets and Institutions: RTC Inspector General*, GGD-95-132R, March 30, 1995, at http://gao.gov/products/GGD-95-132R; and U.S. General Accounting Office, *GPO Office of Inspector General: Alleged Mismanagement and Misconduct by Assistant Inspector General for Audits*, OSI97-3R, April 23, 1997, http://gao.gov/products/OSI-97-3R.

[50] Project on Government Oversight, *Inspectors General: Accountability is a Balancing Act*, 2009, March 20, 2009, pp. 10-11, at http://www.pogoarchives.org/m/go/ig/accountability/ig-accountability-20090320.pdf.

[51] Ibid.

[52] Special IGs include those established by a statute outside of the IG Act. Special IGs include the IG for the Central Intelligence Agency, the IG for the Intelligence Community, the Special Inspector General for Afghanistan Reconstruction, and the Special Inspector General for the Troubled Asset Relief Program.

[53] The five legislative branch IGs include the IGs for the Architect of the Capitol, the Government Accountability Office, the Government Printing Office, the Library of Congress, and the U.S. Capitol Police.

In: Federal Inspectors General
Editor: Emmett Cruz

ISBN: 978-1-63485-524-2


*Chapter 4*

# Inspectors General: Oversight of Small Federal Agencies and the Role of the Inspectors General*

***Beryl H. Davis,***
***Government Accountability Office***

## Why GAO Did This Study

The IGs play a key role in federal agency oversight by enhancing government accountability and protecting the government's resources. This includes a strong leadership role in making recommendations to improve the effectiveness and efficiency of government offices and programs at a time when they are needed most.

This testimony focuses on (1) the creation of independent IG offices, (2) IG oversight of small agencies, and (3) IG independence and budgetary resources.

* This is an edited, reformatted and augmented version of a report, GAO-14-503T, issued by the U.S. Government Accountability Office, April 10, 2014. This report was originally presented as testimony before the Senate Committee on Homeland Security and Governmental Affairs, Subcommittee on Financial and Contracting Oversight for a hearing on "Oversight of Small Agencies". Beryl Davis is Director of Financial Management and Assurance at the GAO.

This testimony provides updates of current IG responsibilities; provisions of the IG Act, as amended; and draws on prior GAO reports and testimonies conducted in accordance with GAO's Quality Assurance Framework.

GAO has made numerous observations and provided matters for the Congress to consider in prior reports when addressing IG oversight at small federal agencies and IG independence.

## WHAT GAO FOUND

The Inspector General Act of 1978, as amended (IG Act), originally established inspectors general (IG) appointed by the President and confirmed by the Senate in 12 major departments and agencies of the government to conduct and supervise independent audits and investigations; recommend policies to promote economy, efficiency, and effectiveness; and prevent and detect fraud and abuse in their departments' and agencies' programs and operations. Based in part on GAO's findings that the internal audit offices of small federal agencies lacked independence and provided inadequate coverage of important programs, the Congress passed the IG Act Amendments of 1988 to establish IGs in designated federal entities (DFE), which are generally smaller agencies established in various statutes as commissions, boards, authorities, corporations, endowments, foundations, institutions, agencies, and administrations identified by the act. The DFE IGs are appointed by their respective entity heads with duties and responsibilities similar to those of IGs appointed by the President. The Congress used a budget threshold of $100 million to help determine which DFEs should have IGs. However, additional DFEs below this threshold were also included for specific reasons.

Significant federal programs and agencies should be subject to oversight by independent IGs; however, small IG offices with limited resources might not have the ability to obtain the technical skills and expertise needed to provide adequate, cost-effective oversight. GAO has previously found that alternative approaches exist to achieve IG oversight that may be appropriate for federal agencies with small budgets and few resources. For example, GAO has recommended on a case-by-case basis that specific small agencies could benefit by obtaining IG oversight from another agency's IG office where the missions of the two agencies are somewhat similar.

Independence is one of the most important elements of an effective IG function. The IG Act, as amended, provides specific protections to IG independence. The IG Reform Act of 2008 further enhanced the IGs' independence by providing specified pay levels, IG legal counsel, a process for handling allegations of IG wrong-doing, and required notification to the Congress before an IG is removed or transferred. The IG Reform Act also requires the IGs' budget requests to be visible in the budget of the U.S. government submitted by the President to the Congress. Additional provisions to enhance the independence of IGs in DFEs with boards or commissions were included in the Dodd-Frank Wall Street Reform and Consumer Protection Act of 2010. Specifically, these IGs are to report organizationally to the entire board or commission rather than a single chairperson. In addition, the IG Act requires a two-thirds majority of the board or commission to remove the IG.

* * *

Chairman McCaskill, Ranking Member Johnson, and Members of the Subcommittee:

I am pleased to be here today to discuss the oversight of federal agencies with relatively small budgets and resources and the role of the inspectors general (IG). IG offices play a key role in federal agency oversight by enhancing government accountability and protecting the government's resources. This includes a strong leadership role in recommending improvements to the effectiveness and efficiency of government offices and programs at a time when they are needed most. The Inspector General Act of 1978, as amended (IG Act), established IG offices at major departments and agencies to conduct and supervise audits and investigations; recommend policies to promote economy, efficiency, and effectiveness; and prevent and detect fraud and abuse in their departments' and agencies' programs and operations.[1]

My testimony today focuses on (1) an overview of the creation of independent IG offices, (2) IG oversight of small agencies, and (3) IG independence and budgetary resources. In preparing this testimony, we included updates of current IG responsibilities and provisions of the IG Act and relied on our prior work related to these issues. More detail on our scope and methodology is included in each issued product. The work on which this testimony is based was conducted in accordance with all sections of GAO's Quality Assurance Framework that are relevant to our objectives. The framework requires that we plan and perform the engagement to meet our stated objectives and that we discuss any limitations in our work. We believe that the information and data obtained, and the analysis conducted, provide a reasonable basis for any findings and conclusions in this product. See the specific reports cited throughout this testimony for information on the standards applied.

## OVERVIEW OF THE CREATION OF IG OFFICES

The IG Act originally established IGs appointed by the President and confirmed by the Senate in 12 major departments and agencies of the government in 1978.[2] Since then, additional IGs have been added through a series of amendments to the IG Act. The Inspector General Act Amendments of 1988 established IGs appointed by their respective entity heads in designated federal entities (DFE) identified by the act with duties and responsibilities similar to those of IGs appointed by the President.[3] DFEs are generally smaller agencies established in various statutes as commissions, boards, authorities, corporations, endowments, foundations, institutions, agencies, and administrations.[4]

Prior to the 1988 amendments, both GAO and the President's Council on Integrity and Efficiency, which preceded the Council of Inspectors General on Integrity and Efficiency (CIGIE), had found that the internal audit offices of small federal agencies lacked independence and provided inadequate coverage of important programs that could benefit from independent oversight by an IG.[5] Additional criteria used by the Congress to determine where to establish these new IG offices included a budget threshold of at least $100 million for the DFEs. Specifically, those agencies with an annual budget of $100 million or greater were considered for inclusion in the 1988 amendments. However, other agencies below this budget threshold were also included for specific reasons. While the IGs in DFEs generally have the same authorities and responsibilities as those established by the 1978 IG Act, there is a clear distinction—they are appointed and removed by their agency heads rather than by the President and are not subject to Senate confirmation.

The 1988 amendments established a new category of "federal entity," which is defined to exclude departments and agencies and DFEs with statutory IGs under the IG Act, as well as judicial and legislative branch entities and others as specified. Further, the 1988 amendments require the Office of Management and Budget (OMB), in consultation with GAO, to annually publish a list of (1) DFEs and, for DFEs that are not boards or commissions, their DFE heads and (2) the federal entities, as that term is defined by the IG Act. OMB's list of DFEs and federal entities is to be published annually in the

Federal Register.[6] The 1988 amendments also require that federal entities, which are defined to exclude entities with a statutory IG under the IG Act, report annually by October 31 to each House of the Congress and to OMB on, among other things, the audit and investigative activities in their respective organizations.

The IGs appointed by the President are generally located in the largest departments and agencies of the government; the DFEs generally have smaller budgets and their IGs have correspondingly smaller budgets and fewer staff members. In our 2011 report of survey results of the IG community, [7] we found 30 departments and agencies with IGs appointed by the President, 33 DFEs with IGs, and 10 IGs established by various statutes similar to the IG Act that were not included in our survey The presidentially appointed IGs and the DFE IGs reported to us total budget authority for fiscal year 2010 of about $2.2 billion with approximately 13,000 authorized full-time equivalent staff (FTE). The presidentially appointed IGs' budget authority constituted about 84 percent of the total IG budget authority and about 86 percent of the total IGs' FTEs.

## IG Oversight of Small Agencies

GAO has long supported the creation of independent IG offices in appropriate federal departments, agencies, and entities, and we continue to believe that significant federal programs and entities should be subject to oversight by independent IGs. At the same time, we have reported some concerns about creating and maintaining small IG offices with limited resources, where an IG might not have the ability to obtain the technical skills and expertise needed to provide adequate and cost-effective oversight. In the final analysis, the determination of whether to place IGs in specific agencies is a policy decision to be decided by the Congress.[8] As a result, we believe there are alternative approaches that the Congress may wish to consider to achieve IG oversight that is appropriate for federal agencies with relatively small budgets and resources. For example, we have recommended, on a case-by-case basis, that specific small agencies could benefit by obtaining IG oversight from another agency's IG office where the missions of the two agencies are somewhat similar. The following provides examples from our previously issued reports on alternatives suggested for IG oversight of small agencies.

- **Export-Import Bank.** In 2001, we were asked to review the need for an IG at the Export-Import Bank, which was defined by OMB as a federal entity under the IG Act, and was not subject to IG oversight. 9 We found that the Export-Import Bank obtained an annual financial audit from an independent public accountant and received additional audits of administrative operations from its internal audit group. We also found that the Export-Import Bank had the largest budget of all other federal entities on OMB's list at the time, and that it was comparable in size to both departments and agencies with IGs appointed by the President and with DFEs with IGs appointed by the head of the DFE. The alternatives we provided for IG oversight of the Export-Import Bank included (1) establishing a new IG office through an amendment to the IG Act with an IG appointed by either the President or by the Export-Import Bank Chairman of the Board of Directors; (2) designating through legislation an existing IG office to provide oversight, such as the Agency for International Development IG; and (3) implementing a memorandum of understanding, which acts like a contract for outside IG services and would not require an amendment to the IG Act or other legislation. Subsequently, the Congress amended the IG Act in 2002 to establish a statutory IG for the Export-Import Bank, appointed by the President and confirmed by the Senate.[10]
- **Chemical Safety and Hazard Investigation Board (CSB).** In 2008, we reported on the responsiveness of CSB to past IG recommendations.[11] We concluded that after 10 years of operations, CSB continued to operate in noncompliance with its statutory mandates by not investigating all accidental chemical releases that involved a fatality, serious injury, or substantial property damage. Since fiscal year 2004, CSB had been obtaining IG oversight services from the Environmental Protection Agency (EPA) IG through a temporary statutory mandate included in its annual appropriation.[12] However, because of the significant issues uncovered by our review, we provided for congressional consideration alternative oversight mechanisms that could be achieved either by amending CSB's authorizing statute or by amending the IG Act to permanently give the EPA IG the authority to serve as the oversight body for CSB and to provide appropriations and staff allocations specifically for the audit function of CSB through a direct line in the EPA appropriation. Alternatives such as allowing CSB to contract for its own oversight or

create an internal audit and investigative unit were not considered as options because of the potential limitations of contracting in terms of both audit independence and the potentially limited duration of the contracting relationship and due to the limited staffing that could reasonably be allocated to an internal oversight function at an agency of its size. The EPA IG has reported continuing oversight efforts at CSB in recent semiannual reports to the Congress.[13]

- **National Mediation Board (NMB).** In a recent example, our mandated review of the programs and management practices at NMB concluded in a 2013 report that the board is a small agency, but with a vital role in facilitating labor relations in the nation's railroads and airlines. [14] We found that NMB's strategic plan lacked assurance that its limited resources were effectively targeted toward the highest priorities. In addition, NMB lacked certain internal controls that could help achieve results and minimize operational problems. We also concluded that in addition to the periodic oversight by GAO and the annual audits of NMB's financial statements by independent public accountants, an existing IG office assigned with the responsibility for providing ongoing audits and investigations of NMB and its operations would result in more effective oversight. We provided a matter for congressional consideration, which discussed the authorization of an appropriate federal agency's IG office to provide independent audit and investigative oversight of NMB.

There are a number of examples where IGs in federal departments and agencies with relatively large budgets currently provide oversight of federal entities with relatively small budgets. To illustrate, the Department of State IG has oversight authority for the Broadcasting Board of Governors. [15] In another example, the Agency for International Development IG provides oversight to several small federal entities, specifically the Millennium Challenge Corporation,[16] the U.S. African Development Foundation, the Inter-American Foundation,[17] and the Overseas Private Investment Corporation.[18] Finally, the Department of Transportation IG is authorized to provide oversight of the National Transportation Safety Board.[19]

## IG Independence and Budgetary Resources

Independence is the cornerstone of professional auditing and one of the most important elements of an effective IG function. The IG Act provides specific protections to IG independence that are unprecedented for an audit and investigative function located within the organization being reviewed. These protections are necessary in large part because of the unusual reporting requirements of the IGs, who are subject to the general supervision of their agency heads and are also expected to provide independent reports of their work externally to the Congress.

The IG Act provides the IGs with independence by authorizing them to select and employ their own staffs, make such investigations and reports as they deem necessary, and report the results of their work directly to the Congress. In addition, the IG Act provides the IGs with a right of access to information, and prohibits interference with IG audits or investigations by agency personnel. The act further provides the IGs with the duty to inform the Attorney General of suspected violations of federal criminal law.

With the growing complexity of the federal government, the severity of the problems it faces, and the fiscal constraints under which it operates, it is important that an independent, objective, and reliable IG structure be in place where appropriate in the federal government to ensure adequate audit and investigative coverage. The IG Act provides each IG with the ability to exercise judgment in the use of independence protections specified in the act; therefore, the ultimate success or failure of an IG office is largely determined by the individual IG placed in that office and that person's ability to maintain independence both in fact and appearance.[20]

The Congress passed the IG Reform Act of 2008 (Reform Act) to further enhance IG independence and accountability.[21] Among other provisions, the Reform Act requires the rate of basic pay of the IGs appointed by the President to be at a specified level, and for the DFE IGs, at or above that of a majority of other senior-level executives at their entities. The Reform Act also requires an IG to obtain legal advice from his or her own counsel or to obtain counsel from another IG office or from CIGIE. Additionally, the act provides a statutory process for handling allegations of wrongdoing by IGs so that such reviews are not done by the same management officials who are subject to IG oversight. The act also requires both the President and the DFE heads to give written reasons to the Congress for removing or transferring an IG at least 30 days prior to the action.

The Reform Act also increased the visibility of the IGs' budgetary resources through the annual budget process. Specifically, the act requires that IG budget requests include certain information and be separately identified in the President's budget submission to the Congress. In addition, along with the separately identified IG budgets, an IG may include comments with respect to the budget if the amount of the IG budget submitted by the agency or the President would substantially inhibit the IG from performing the duties of the office. These budget provisions are intended to help ensure adequate funding and additional independence of IG budgets by providing the Congress with transparency into the funding of each agency's IG while not interfering with the agency head's or the President's right to formulate and transmit their own budget amounts for the IG.

In 2010, the Dodd-Frank Wall Street Reform and Consumer Protection Act (Dodd-Frank Act) amended the IG Act with provisions to enhance the independence of IGs in DFEs with boards or commissions.[22] Specifically, the Dodd-Frank Act changed who would be considered the head of certain DFEs for purposes of IG appointment, general supervision, and reporting under the IG Act. If the DFE has a board or commission, the IG Act now requires each of these IGs to report organizationally to the entire board or commission as the head of the DFE rather than an individual chairman. In addition, the IG Act requires the written concurrence of a two-thirds majority of the board or commission to remove an IG. Prior to this protection, most DFE IGs reported to, and were subject to removal by, the individual serving as head of the DFE.

In other past legislative reforms, the Congress has taken actions to convert IGs from appointment by the agency heads to appointment by the President with Senate confirmation as a way to enhance IG independence. For example, on the heels of the savings and loan and banking crisis over two decades ago, the role of the Federal Deposit Insurance Corporation's (FDIC) IG became increasingly important in providing oversight. Because of the perceived limitation of the FDIC IG's independence resulting from agency appointment, the Congress converted the IG from agency appointment to appointment by the President with Senate confirmation.[23] In another example, the Congress took action to convert the Tennessee Valley Authority (TVA) IG to appointment by the President with Senate confirmation because of concerns about interference by TVA management.[24] In both cases, Congress recognized that the IG's independence would be enhanced by the presidential appointment.

## Concluding Observations

IGs play a critical role in federal oversight and we believe that all significant federal programs and entities should be subject to oversight by IGs. We have supported the creation of additional IG offices and the enhancements to their independence by past legislation. However, we continue to have some concerns about creating and maintaining IG offices in relatively small federal agencies where it may not be cost-effective to obtain the skills and expertise needed to provide adequate oversight. We believe there are alternatives to creating additional IG offices that can be both effective and less costly. These alternatives for oversight should be decided on a case-by-case basis depending on the critical nature of the small agencies' missions and the risks identified that require increased oversight. Because the Congress relies on the IGs to provide current information about their respective agencies' programs and activities, the determination of where and how to provide IG oversight in specific agencies is a policy decision addressed best by the Congress.

This concludes my formal statement. Chairman McCaskill, Ranking Member Johnson, and Members of the Subcommittee, I would be pleased to answer any questions that you or the Subcommittee members may have at this time.

## End Notes

[1] Pub. L. No. 95-452, 92 Stat. 1101 (Oct. 12, 1978), *codified, as amended*, at 5 U.S.C. App.

[2] In 1978, 12 IGs were established by the IG Act at the Departments of Agriculture, Commerce, Housing and Urban Development, the Interior, Labor, and Transportation; and at the Community Services Administration (which has since been abolished), Environmental Protection Agency, General Services Administration, National Aeronautics and Space Administration, Small Business Administration, and Veterans Administration (now the Department of Veterans Affairs).

[3] Pub. L. No. 100-504, 102 Stat. 2515 (Oct. 18, 1988).

[4] In addition to IGs established by amendments to the IG Act, we reported in 2011 that there were 10 IG offices established by various other statutes similar to the IG Act. They are the IG offices at the Architect of the Capitol, Central Intelligence Agency, Government Accountability Office, Government Printing Office, Library of Congress, Office of the Director of National Intelligence, Special Inspector General for Afghanistan Reconstruction, Special Inspector General for Iraq Reconstruction, Special Inspector General for the Troubled Asset Relief Program, and U.S. Capitol Police. (GAO, *Inspectors General: Reporting on Independence, Effectiveness, and Expertise*, GAO-11-770 (Washington, D.C.: Sept. 21. 2011). The Special Inspector General for Iraq Reconstruction terminated its operations as of September 30, 2013.

[5] CIGIE was established by the Inspector General Reform Act of 2008, Pub. L. 110-409, 122 Stat. 4302 (Oct. 14, 2008), to replace the President's Council on Integrity and Efficiency and the Executive Council on Integrity and Efficiency, which had been established by executive orders. CIGIE consists mainly of IGs, to address integrity, economy, and effectiveness issues that transcend individual government agencies, and to increase the professionalism and effectiveness of personnel in the IG offices.

[6] OMB published its most recent list on January 14, 2014. 79 Fed. Reg. 1896.

[7] GAO-11-770.

[8] GAO, *U.S. Export-Import Bank: Views on Inspector General Oversight*, GAO-01-1038R (Washington, D.C.: Sept. 6, 2001).

[9] GAO-01-1038R.

[10] Pub. L. No. 107-189, § 22(a)(c)(d), 116 Stat. 707,708 (June 14, 2002).

[11] GAO, *Chemical Safety Board: Improvements in Management and Oversight Are Needed*, GAO-08-864R (Washington, D.C.: Aug. 22, 2008).

[12] *See, e.g.,* Consolidated Appropriations Act, 2004, Pub. L. 108-199, 118 Stat. 3, 399 (Jan. 23, 2004): Regarding CSB oversight, "*Provided, further,* That notwithstanding any other provision of law, the individual appointed to the position of Inspector General of the Environmental Protection Agency (EPA) shall, by virtue of such appointment, also hold the position of Inspector General of the Board: *Provided further,* That notwithstanding any other provision of law, the Inspector General of the Board shall utilize personnel of the Office of Inspector General of EPA in performing the duties of the Inspector General of the Board, and shall not appoint any individuals to positions within the Board."

[13] Environmental Protection Agency Office of Inspector General, *Semiannual Report to Congress April 1, 2013 – September 30, 2013*, EPA-350-R-13-003 (Washington, D.C.: November 2013), and *Semiannual Report to Congress October 1, 2012 – March 31, 2013*, EPA-350-R-13-001 (Washington, D.C.: May 2013).

[14] GAO, *National Mediation Board: Strengthening Planning and Controls Could Better Facilitate Rail and Air Labor Relations*, GAO-14-5 (Washington, D.C.: Dec. 3, 2013).

[15] Foreign Affairs Reform and Restructuring Act of 1998, Pub. L. No. 105-277, div. G, § 1314, 112 Stat. 2681-761, 2681-776-77 (Oct. 21, 1998), *classified at* 22 U.S.C § 6533.

[16] Millennium Challenge Corporation Act, Pub. L. No. 108-199, title VI, § 614(f)(1), 118 Stat. 211, 223 (Jan. 23, 2004), *classified at* 22 U.S.C. § 7713(f)(1).

[17] Consolidated Appropriations Act, 2000, Pub. L. No. 106-133, div. B, § 1000(a)(7), 113 Stat. 1501, 1536, Appendix G, § 205, 113 Stat. 1501, 1501A-422 (Nov. 29, 1999), *codified at* 5 U.S.C. appx. 8A(f)(a).

[18] The Agency for International Development has provided IG oversight to the Overseas Private Investment Corporation pursuant to the interagency agreement that is in effect at the time the oversight services are rendered.

[19] National Transportation Safety Board Amendments Act of 2000, Pub. L. No. 106-424, § 12, 114 Stat. 1883, 1887 (Nov. 1, 2000), *codified, as amended, at* 49 U.S.C. §1137.

[20] GAO, *Inspectors General: Opportunities to Enhance Independence and Accountability*, GAO-07-1089T (Washington, D.C.: July 11, 2007).

[21] Pub. L. No 110-409, 122 Stat. 4302 (Oct. 14, 2008).

[22] Pub. L. No. 111-203, §§ 989B-D,1081, 124 Stat. 1376, 1945-46, 2080 (July 21, 2010).

[23] Resolution Trust Corporation Completion Act, Pub. L. No.103-204, § 23, 107 Stat.2369, 2407-08 (Dec. 17, 1993). To increase the independence of the entity's IG, this act converted the FDIC IG from appointment by the head of FDIC to appointment by the President with Senate confirmation.

[24] Pub. L. No. 106-422, § 1, 114 Stat. 1872 (Nov. 1, 2000). To obtain increased IG independence, this act converted the TVA IG from appointment by the head of TVA to appointment by the President with Senate confirmation.

In: Federal Inspectors General
Editor: Emmett Cruz

ISBN: 978-1-63485-524-2


*Chapter 5*

# STATEMENT OF MICHAEL E. HOROWITZ, INSPECTOR GENERAL, U.S. DEPARTMENT OF JUSTICE. HEARING ON "INSPECTORS GENERAL: INDEPENDENCE, ACCESS AND AUTHORITY"*

Mr. Chairman, Congressman Cummings, and Members of the Committee:

Thank you for inviting me to testify regarding the continued challenges to the independence, access, and authority of Inspectors General. During my nearly three years as the Inspector General of the Department of Justice (DOJ OIG), I have faced several challenges in these areas. Among the most serious is the continued refusal by the Department to recognize that Section 6(a) of the Inspector General Act authorizes the DOJ OIG to obtain access to all records in the Department's possession that we need in order to perform our oversight responsibilities.

In January, I also became the Chair of the Council of the Inspectors General on Integrity and Efficiency (CIGIE), and I am honored to serve the Inspector General community in that position. As DOJ Inspector General and CIGIE Chair, I look forward to working with this Committee to ensure that Inspectors General have the independence and tools they need to do their jobs on behalf of the American people, including making sure they have complete

* This is an edited, reformatted and augmented version of a statement presented February 3, 2015 before the House Committee on Oversight and Government Reform.

and timely access to agency information that is critical to performing their mission. We appreciate the bipartisan legislation in this area that was proposed by this Committee last year, and we look forward to continuing our work with the Committee to assist you in developing the legislative reforms that will help improve our ability to conduct strong and effective oversight.

## ACHIEVEMENTS OF INSPECTORS GENERAL

Year in and year out, the Inspector General community has demonstrated its ability to root out waste, fraud, abuse, mismanagement, and misconduct through our audits, investigations, inspections, and reviews. Our efforts result in agencies that are more effective and efficient. The foundation for this work is our independence and central to that is our ability to access information that is in the possession of the agencies that we each oversee.

Inspectors General have a track record of delivering measurable and significant benefits to the taxpayers. For example, in FY 2013, the approximately 14,000 employees at the 72 federal Offices of Inspector General (OIG) conducted audits, inspections, evaluations, and investigations resulting in the identification of approximately $37 billion in potential cost savings and approximately $14.8 billion from investigative recoveries and receivables. In comparison, the aggregate FY 2013 budget of the 72 federal OIGs was approximately $2.5 billion, meaning that these potential savings represent about a $21 return on every dollar invested in the OIGs, in addition to the other valuable guidance we provide in the management of our agencies' operations and programs. And all of this was accomplished during a time of sequestration, when many of us in the Inspector General community, including the DOJ OIG, were faced with significant budget cuts that directly impacted our work. For example, staffing in my office fell by nearly ten percent, which inevitably affected our workflow, and is still below pre-sequestration levels. As we once again face the prospect of sequestration next year, many of us in the Inspector General community are concerned about the potential impact that another period of sharply limited resources could have on our ability to continue to perform the kind and range of audits, inspections, evaluations, and investigations that are expected of us.

Speaking specifically for my Office, the DOJ OIG also has delivered outstanding value to the taxpayer. In FY 2014, the DOJ OIG identified over $23 million in questioned costs and nearly $1.3 million in taxpayer funds that could be put to better use by the Department. And our criminal, civil, and administrative investigations resulted in the imposition or identification of almost $7 million in fines, restitution, recoveries, and other monetary results last fiscal year. This is in addition to the $136 million in audit-related findings and over $51 million in investigative-related findings that the DOJ OIG identified from FY 2009 through FY 2013. These monetary savings and recoveries, however, do not take into account some of our most significant reviews, which cannot be translated into quantifiable dollar savings but which address fundamental issues affecting national security, civil liberties, safety and security at federal prisons, effectiveness of law enforcement programs, and the conduct of Department employees. Examples include our reviews of the FBI's use of its authorities under the Patriot Act and the FISA Amendments Act, the government's information sharing prior to the Boston Marathon bombing, ATF's Operation Fast and Furious, the BOP's management of the compassionate release program, the Department's handling of known or suspected terrorists in the Witness Security Program, the FBI's management of the terrorist watchlist, nepotism by Department personnel, and our investigation of the FBI's corrupt relationship with James "Whitey" Bulger.

In addition, we have taken a number of significant steps during my tenure as DOJ Inspector General to address whistleblower issues, which are critical to ensuring that Department employees are encouraged to report waste, fraud, abuse, and misconduct, and that they can do so without fear of retaliation. The DOJ OIG was instrumental in creating and continues to chair CIGIE's Whistleblower Ombudsmen Working Group. I am proud of the efforts of this CIGIE Working Group and look forward to working with my fellow Inspectors General as CIGIE Chair to continue to move forward on important whistleblower issues.

## CHALLENGES FACING INSPECTORS GENERAL

While the Inspector General community has been able to generate impressive results, we face significant issues and challenges. For example, timely access to information in our agency's files remains an important issue and challenge. As I have testified on multiple occasions, in order to conduct effective oversight, an IG must have timely and complete access to documents and materials needed for its audits, reviews, and investigations. This is an issue of utmost importance, as evidenced by the fact that 47 Inspectors

General signed a letter in August 2014 to the Congress strongly endorsing the principle of unimpaired Inspector General access to agency records.

The Inspector General Act could not be clearer – Inspectors General are entitled to complete, timely, and unfiltered access to all documents and records within the agency's possession. Delaying or denying access to agency documents imperils an IG's independence, and impedes our ability to provide the effective and independent oversight that saves taxpayers money and improves the operations of the federal government. Actions that limit, condition, or delay access have profoundly negative consequences for our work: they make us less effective, encourage other agencies to take similar actions in the future, and erode the morale of the dedicated professionals that make up our staffs.

My Office knows these problems all too well, and we continue to face challenges in getting timely access to information from Department components. In particular, the FBI continues to take the position it first raised in 2010 that Section 6(a) of the Inspector General Act (IG Act) does not entitle the DOJ OIG to all records in the FBI's possession and therefore has refused DOJ OIG requests for various types of records. As I have indicated in my prior testimony before this Committee, the DOJ OIG and CIGIE strenuously disagree with the FBI's position, which we have both made clear to the Department's leadership.

In May 2014, in an attempt to resolve this dispute, the Department's leadership asked the Office of Legal Counsel to issue an opinion addressing the legal objections raised by the FBI. However, over eight months later, we are still waiting for that opinion even though, in our view, this matter is straightforward and could have been resolved by the Department's leadership without requesting an opinion from OLC. I cannot emphasize enough how important it is that OLC issue its opinion promptly because the existing process at the Department, which as described below essentially assumes the correctness of the FBI's legal position, undermines our independence by requiring us to seek permission from the Department's leadership in order to access certain records. The status quo cannot be allowed to continue indefinitely.

We appreciate the strong bipartisan support we have received from Congress in trying to address these serious issues. Most significantly, in December 2014, a provision was included in the Fiscal Year 2015 appropriations law – Section 218 – which prohibits the Justice Department from using appropriated funds to deny, prevent, or impede the DOJ OIG's timely access to records, documents, and other materials in the Department's possession, unless it is in accordance with an express limitation of Section 6(a) of the Inspector General Act. While the law only recently went into effect, it is clear that the Department has taken notice of it and it has already had an impact on our ability to get access to records in certain reviews.

However, despite Congress's reaffirmation in Section 218 of its support for DOJ OIG's access to records in the Department's possession, the FBI continues to maintain that Section 6(a) of the IG Act does not authorize access to certain records in its possession, such as grand jury, Title III electronic surveillance, and Fair Credit Reporting Act information, because of disclosure limitations in statutes other than the IG Act. As a result, the FBI is continuing the costly and time-consuming process it put in place prior to Section 218's enactment of reviewing documents responsive to DOJ OIG requests prior to producing them to us. The FBI has been undertaking this process in order to withhold from the DOJ OIG records that the FBI believes we are not legally entitled to receive, despite the absence of any such limitation in the IG Act. Prior to the enactment of Section 218, this FBI document review process, in addition to consuming the FBI's resources, significantly impacted the FBI's timely production of material to us in several of our matters, including whistleblower retaliation investigations. As we are directed to do by Section 218, the DOJ OIG will be reporting to Congress impediments imposed by the FBI, or any DOJ component, to our timely access to records in the Department's possession that we are entitled to receive under Section 6(a) of the IG Act.

It is time to resolve this legal dispute. The FBI's position that Section 6(a) of the IG Act does not authorize the DOJ OIG to have access to various categories of records in its possession contradicts the plain language of the IG Act, Congress's clear intent when it created the DOJ OIG (as confirmed by the recent enactment of Section 218), the FBI's and the Department's practice prior to 2010 of frequently providing the very same categories of information to the DOJ OIG without any legal objection, court decisions by two different federal District Judges in 1998 and 1999 stating that the DOJ OIG could receive grand jury material, and the reasoning of a 1984 decision by the Office of Legal Counsel concluding that grand jury material could be provided to the Department's Office of Professional Responsibility.

The Department, in response to the FBI's questioning of our legal authority to review these types of records, has imposed a process whereby the Attorney General or the Deputy Attorney General may grant permission to the DOJ OIG to access such records if they conclude that specific reviews will assist them in the performance of their duties, and they have done so in each such review so far where the issue has arisen. However, no such permission is necessary under Section 6(a) of the Inspector General Act. Moreover, requiring an OIG to obtain permission from agency leadership in order to review agency documents seriously impairs Inspector General independence, creates excessive delays, and may lead to incomplete, inaccurate, or significantly delayed findings or recommendations.

We remain hopeful that the OLC opinion that has been sought by the Department's leadership will conclude that the IG Act entitles the OIG to independent access to the records and information to which we are entitled under the express terms of the IG Act. This will be one of the first topics that I intend to discuss with the Department's new leadership. However, should OLC interpret the IG Act in a manner that undercuts Congress's clear intent and limits the DOJ OIG's access to documents, I would be pleased to work with the Committee to develop a legislative remedy to address this issue.

Let me briefly mention other areas where I personally think the ability of Inspectors General to conduct strong and effective oversight could be enhanced. I expect that CIGIE will shortly be providing the Congress with a letter identifying the legislative priorities for the entire Inspector General community.

One such area is the capacity of Inspectors General to obtain testimony from former agency employees, contractors, and grant recipients. While the IG Act provides us with the ability to subpoena documents and records from those individuals, we are unable to require them to provide testimony, even if they have critical evidence of fraud or of agency misconduct. I have seen several instances during my tenure as Inspector General where former employees of the Department (including those who resigned or retired immediately prior to a DOJ OIG interview), contractors, and grant recipients have refused to speak with the DOJ OIG, thereby impeding our ability to gather potentially valuable and relevant evidence. While I believe any authority granting Inspectors General the ability to compel testimony should include protections to ensure the authority is used appropriately and only when necessary, and that it does not inadvertently impair Justice Department prosecutions, I am confident based on my years as a former federal prosecutor and as a senior official in the Department's Criminal Division that such protections can readily be developed while also empowering Inspectors General to carry out their responsibilities. I look forward to discussing this issue further with the Committee.

Another area where legislation could enhance the ability of Inspectors General to conduct strong and effective oversight is in addressing the limitations on our ability to obtain and match readily available information across Executive Branch agencies in furtherance of our efforts to combat fraud and misconduct. These limitations arise out of the Computer Matching and Privacy Protection Act (CMPPA). The information at issue currently exists within the possession of government agencies – it does not require any further collection of documents or information – and Inspectors General of the agency are already entitled to access it under the IG Act. Yet the CMPPA contains provisions that impact the ability of Inspectors General to efficiently obtain information from another agency and to share it with each other. The timely use of such data by Inspectors General to identify those who improperly receive federal assistance, federal grants or contracts, or duplicative payments will improve program efficiency, enhance recovery of improper payments, and empower Inspectors General to better address waste, fraud, and abuse in federal programs. In my view, exempting Inspectors General from the CMPPA would greatly assist our ability to ensure that federal programs are effective and efficient without undermining the purposes of that law.

Finally, I am aware of the recent questions that have been raised relating to the work of CIGIE's Integrity Committee, including with respect to the timeliness of its work and the transparency of its efforts. One of my first meetings as Chair of CIGIE was with the Assistant Director of the FBI, who chairs the Integrity Committee, in order to discuss ways to address these issues. OIGs must maintain the highest levels of accountability and integrity, and as Chair of CIGIE I will make it a top priority to improve the procedures for the Integrity Committee.

## CONCLUSION

In conclusion, I look forward to working closely with this Committee to ensure that Inspectors General continue to be empowered to provide the kind of independent and objective oversight for which they have become known, and which the taxpayers deserve. This concludes my prepared statement, and I will be happy to answer any questions the Committee may have.

In: Federal Inspectors General
Editor: Emmett Cruz
ISBN: 978-1-63485-524-2


*Chapter 6*

# STATEMENT OF ARTHUR A. ELKINS JR., INSPECTOR GENERAL, U.S. ENVIRONMENTAL PROTECTION AGENCY. HEARING ON "INSPECTORS GENERAL: INDEPENDENCE, ACCESS AND AUTHORITY"*

Good morning, Chairman Chaffetz, Ranking Member Cummings and members of the committee. I am Arthur Elkins, Inspector General (IG) at the U.S. Environmental Protection Agency (EPA). Thank you for inviting me to appear before you today. I appeared before this committee on June 19, 2014, to address impediments to access at the U.S. Chemical Safety and Hazard Investigation Board (CSB), for which I also am the IG, and again on September 10, 2014, to address broader issues of access and whether there is a need to strengthen or clarify the Inspector General Act to address impediments and access issues. Today, I would like to report to you on the progress we have made since those hearings and the challenges that still remain.

Before I begin, I would like to publicly commend the expertise, dedication, diligence and professionalism of Office of Inspector General (OIG) staff—not only at the EPA, but across the federal government—who work hard each day to carry out our very important mission of promoting economy,

* This is an edited, reformatted and augmented version of a statement presented February 3, 2015 before the House Committee on Oversight and Government Reform.

efficiency and effectiveness; and preventing and detecting fraud, waste and abuse through independent oversight of programs and operations.

## Overview of the EPA OIG

The EPA OIG is charged with conducting investigations and audits related to programs and operations at the EPA and CSB. The EPA OIG operates with a separate budget and decisionmaking authority, and neither EPA nor CSB senior leaders may prohibit, prevent or obstruct us from conducting our work.

### CSB Has Substantially (But Not Fully) Complied with the OIG Requests

First, with regard to the CSB officials' refusal to provide documents, you will recall that we had requested certain documents in the course of an investigation. CSB officials refused to provide them, asserting that the denial was based on attorney/client privilege. However, we explained that such denial violated the IG Act, specifically Section 6(a)(1), which provides for the IG's unfettered access to all materials and information available to the agency. After more than a year of refusals by the CSB, I sent a "Seven Day letter"—a tool provided for in the IG Act—to Chairman Rafael Moure-Eraso. A Seven Day Letter requires the agency head to transmit the IG's letter and the agency's response to appropriate committees or subcommittees of Congress within seven calendar days. Although the CSB did forward my letter to committees, including this one, CSB officials continued to refuse to produce the documents.

At the June 2014 hearing before this committee, the Chairman and Ranking Member both instructed the CSB to provide the documents that the OIG sought. The CSB substantially complied with those instructions; however, they have yet to provide an affirmation of full compliance with our requests. To elaborate, in August 2014, the OIG asked Chairman Moure-Eraso and other senior CSB officials to affirm their methodology for searching and identifying documents within the scope of OIG's requests, and that they had fully complied with the requests. At this time, none of the CSB officials have done so.

While the OIG cannot attest to the receipt of all requested documents from the CSB, as explained above, we were able to proceed with and complete our investigation. Last week, I sent the OIG's report of investigative results to President Obama, as there is no one higher than Chairman Moure-Eraso at the CSB, and he is appointed by the President. That report finds that there is evidence sufficient to support a conclusion that the Chairman and two of his senior officials violated the Federal Records Act, and implementing regulations, by using non-governmental email systems to conduct official government business and not capturing those emails in the CSB records system.

I would like to thank the committee for taking action in response to our Seven Day Letter, which allowed us to proceed with and conclude our investigation.

## PROGRESS AND REMAINING CHALLENGES REGARDING EPA'S OFFICE OF HOMELAND SECURITY

Next, I will address progress with regard to impediments to the OIG's ability to carry out its functions as imposed by the EPA's Office of Homeland Security (OHS). You will recall that in my testimony at the September 2014 hearing, I advised the committee that the EPA had asserted there was a category of activity defined as "intelligence" to which the OIG may have access only subject to the EPA's granting of permission. This situation impeded the OIG's ability to investigate threats against EPA employees and facilities, conduct certain misconduct investigations and investigate computer intrusions. In addition, OHS was conducting investigative activities of its own, without any legal authority to do so, thereby interfering with—and in some cases fouling—OIG investigations.

Since that hearing, senior OIG officials have met multiple times with senior agency officials to address a range of issues falling under these general categories. We have reached at least a theoretical agreement on a substantial portion of the issues, although I must offer two caveats: first, we are only now beginning to implement agreements, and second, we have not resolved the issue of OHS having a criminal investigator assigned to it while OHS lacks any investigative authority.

What we have agreed upon is that there is no category of activity at the EPA to which OIG does not have unfettered access, as provided by the IG Act. The "intelligence" activities can and are to be shared with the OIG if the OIG seeks access or an issue is within OIG purview. One specific impediment to being able to reach agreement previously was a memorandum of understanding (MOU) that the EPA had entered into unilaterally with the Federal Bureau of Investigation (FBI). The OIG was not party to, nor was it consulted in, creating that MOU. The EPA asserted that the MOU precluded it from sharing information with the OIG.

However, FBI senior management has since confirmed to the EPA that the FBI does not require withholding information from the OIG, and the EPA has confirmed to the OIG that it will now share the information we had been seeking, both with regard to previous matters and going forward on an ongoing basis. We have yet to have a three-way meeting among the EPA, the OIG and the FBI to confirm all of this, and to rescind or substantially modify the MOU.

With regard to the OHS criminal investigator, we cannot know whether OHS continues to conduct investigative activity.

These are important impediment issues that we have not yet resolved with the agency.

I am pleased to note that on January 2, 2015, Administrator McCarthy sent to the EPA workforce a memorandum addressing cooperation with and providing information to the OIG. She told employees that one of the ways employees can ensure that they all perform at their best is to support the internal review and oversight carried out by the OIG. She noted that the vigilance of EPA staff is key to successful OIG oversight, and she specifically stated that she expects all employees to report fraud, waste and abuse to the OIG if they see it.

## Federal Agencies Lack Enforceable Mechanisms to Compel Employees to Cooperate with the OIG

I trust that these updates on specific matters discussed at previous hearings will help inform the committee's deliberations about any further investigative or legislative actions it may need to take. I would like to close by addressing big-picture challenges that my office, and many other OIGs across government, continue to face.

On August 1, 2014, my office received information from the Security Management Division at the EPA alleging serious employee misconduct by a senior EPA official. The information initially provided alleged that on July 30, 2014, the senior official had engaged in improper behavior with a 21-year-old female intern from another agency.

The investigation into the initial allegation uncovered allegations of several other improper actions by that senior official. The allegations investigated in this case were: (1) the senior official's inappropriate behavior toward at least 16 women, from 2004 to present; (2) violation of security procedures by the senior official; (3) mishandling of classified information by the senior official; and (4) lack of due diligence by other senior EPA executives (by not acting on information about this senior official) that resulted in six additional women being subjected to the senior official's inappropriate behavior from January 2014 to July 2014. During this latter period, the senior official was promoted.

While the OIG had interviewed the senior official during the initial stages of the investigation with the uncovering of information about additional allegations, the OIG determined it needed to interview this official again. By that time, the senior official was on paid administrative leave.

OIG investigators attempted to interview the senior official again on January 12, 2015. However, the senior official declined to cooperate with the OIG investigation and refused to be interviewed, despite EPA supervisors directing the official to cooperate with the OIG. That senior official retired from federal service, that day, after spending approximately five months on paid administrative leave. At that point, the OIG had no further access to the official and the agency had no disciplinary remedies available to it.

In addition to this senior official's unwillingness to cooperate with our administrative investigation, over the last two years, my office has been presented with other situations in which individuals refused to cooperate in administrative interviews. In one case, an Office of General Counsel attorney refused to cooperate with the OIG, even when prompted (although not directed) by the agency to cooperate. To my knowledge, the agency did not take any action against this attorney. Instead the attorney left the agency to work for another federal agency. Another instance involved a GS-15 program advisor in the Office of Research and Development who refused to cooperate with my office as part of an administrative investigation regarding violations of security policies. This case is still pending, but the agency, to my knowledge, has not taken any action against the EPA employee for not cooperating with my office.

As you know, the IG Act at Section 6(a) gives the OIG unfettered access to all information "available" to its department or agency. This authority predominantly has been applied to obtaining documents. But it also applies to access to people. If an OIG determines that it needs to interview an agency employee who may have relevant information, other than in an investigation with possible criminal exposure where the subject would be so advised by the OIG, that employee is obligated to provide the information requested.

But the IG Act provides no remedy for an employee's violation of this obligation. We have had situations where we attempt to interview an employee and the employee refuses. We can and do then tell the agency that it needs to require the employee to comply with the OIG's request. If the employee continues to refuse to comply with both the OIG and the agency, we are left without recourse. Further, in some of the recent cases we have encountered, the employee refuses to be interviewed and then resigns or retires, putting himself or herself permanently beyond the reach of the OIG. Of course, if there is a criminal violation, the employee can still be charged by prosecutors.

I believe that this committee should look into the "gap" between what the IG Act requires and OIGs' ability to achieve those requirements in such circumstances. Subject to constitutional due process rights, there might be ways to strengthen an agency's ability to discipline an employee for failure to comply with an OIG request. For example, Congress could provide for placing the employee on leave without pay status, rather than administrative leave with pay. Alternatively, Congress might consider restricting the availability of appropriated funds to pay the employee.

Finally, I know that this committee has recognized and thanked me personally, and the OIG community generally, for the good work we do in protecting taxpayer funds. We appreciate that.

But, I have to remark on the disconnect between what the oversight committees observe and the appropriations that emerge from Congress as a whole. The budget levels made available to me are impeding our ability to do our work. This is penny-wise and pound-foolish, as Ben Franklin used to say. We returned $7.33 for every dollar given to us in the past year. When the OIG is not able to carry out its responsibilities because of inadequate funding, it is a net loss to the federal government and American taxpayers. I know this is not an appropriations committee, but I ask for any help you can provide us in this regard.

## CONCLUSION

I have discussed today three major risks to OIG independence: access to agency documents; access to agency staff; and adequate funding. All of these are necessary to fully accomplish our mission. Yet the OIGs have control over none of these, nor ultimately can we compel solutions.

All require external cooperation—from the Executive Branch for document and staff access and from the Legislative Branch for funding access. As I stated when I appeared before this committee in September 2014, the concept underlying the IG Act is fragile, and can be likened to a house of cards. The removal of the cooperation card, as related to the key risks I have discussed, will cause the foundation upon which the house is built to collapse.

Mr. Chairman, this concludes my prepared statement. I will be pleased to answer any questions that you or committee members may have.

In: Federal Inspectors General
Editor: Emmett Cruz

ISBN: 978-1-63485-524-2


*Chapter 7*

# TESTIMONY OF KATHY A. BULLER, INSPECTOR GENERAL, U.S. PEACE CORPS. HEARING ON "INSPECTORS GENERAL: INDEPENDENCE, ACCESS AND AUTHORITY"*

Chairman Chaffetz, Ranking Member Cummings, and distinguished members of the Committee:

Thank you for inviting me to appear before you today to discuss the challenges to access and independence faced by my office. I testified on this issue twice last year: on January 15 and again on September 5. While progress was made after each hearing, some challenges remain.

## DENIAL OF ACCESS TO SEXUAL ASSAULT RECORDS

The Peace Corps Office of Inspector General (OIG) access issues stem from a rather sensitive and important subject: the Peace Corps' handling of volunteer reports of sexual assault. So I must emphasize from the outset that our push for access goes beyond our zeal for upholding the basic principle that transparency and accountability are the hallmarks of good governance. Our push for access is about fulfilling our collective responsibility to ensure that we – Congress, the Peace Corps, and OIG – do everything we can to ensure

* This is an edited, reformatted and augmented version of testimony presented February 3, 2015 before the House Committee on Oversight and Government Reform.

our volunteers, who sacrifice so much when serving in remote corners of the world, receive the services they need when they are victims of a sexual assault.

Standing in our way to fulfilling that duty is a legal opinion drafted on July 9, 2013, by the Peace Corps' former general counsel. That legal opinion asserts the Kate Puzey Volunteer Protection Act of 2011(Kate Puzey Act),[1] overrides my broad right of access to agency records under the Inspector General Act of 1978, as amended, (IG Act).[2] As a result of that legal opinion, the agency has implemented policies and procedures denying us access to information.

Since my last testimony on September 5, the Peace Corps has corrected course by issuing policies and procedures that grant OIG greater access to information.[3] It's worth reminding the Committee that these revisions took two years of discussions with the agency and members of Congress, two congressional hearings, negative press coverage, a hold being placed on the nomination of the Director, and, ultimately, the signing of a memorandum of understanding (MOU) between the agency and OIG. Despite this progress, the underlying legal opinion supporting those policies and procedures is still in place and much work remains to be done to undo the damage caused by these access-denying policies.

## SUMMARY OF LEGAL ISSUE

### The IG Act

When Congress enacted the IG Act it recognized that access to information is essential for inspectors general to effectively oversee agency programs and operations. Accordingly, Section 6(a)(1) of the IG Act enables every inspector general to access:

> All records, reports, audits, reviews, documents, papers, recommendations, or other material available to the applicable establishment which relate to programs and operations with respect to which that Inspector General has responsibilities under this Act.

There is no ambiguity in this language. IGs have access to all agency documents and information, and the legislative history to the IG Act leaves no room for doubt: the language 'all records' is expansive and is intended to include even confidential agency memoranda.[4]

## The Kate Puzey Act

Congress enacted the Kate Puzey Act following reports that emerged after the ABC network's 20/20 show aired a story on how the agency mishandled sexual assault complaints by former volunteers. The show also focused on the mishandling of an unrelated complaint filed by Kate Puzey, a volunteer who was murdered in Benin in 2009 after a staff member allegedly failed to keep her complaint confidential.[5]

Section 8E(d)(1)(B) of the Kate Puzey Act provides OIG with key oversight roles in ensuring the agency adequately responds to sexual assault and other crimes; effectively implements and trains on the Sexual Assault Risk Reduction and Response policy and program; and delivers services to sexual assault victims. The Kate Puzey Act requires that OIG conduct an evaluation on this matter and report to Congress by November 21, 2013, and again in 2016.[6] The report must be based on a case review of a statistically significant number of sexual assault cases.[7]

Section 8A(f)(2) of the Kate Puzey Act mandates that victims have access to a restricted reporting mechanism that allows them to receive services without automatically triggering an official investigation. If a victim makes a restricted report, the victim's personally identifiable information (PII) can only be shared with specified individuals unless an exception applies. One of those exceptions authorizes disclosures "to State and Federal courts when ordered, or if disclosure is required by Federal or State statute."

# Summary of Legal Issue

## The IG Act

When Congress enacted the IG Act it recognized that access to information is essential for inspectors general to effectively oversee agency programs and operations. Accordingly, Section 6(a)(1) of the IG Act enables every inspector general to access:

> All records, reports, audits, reviews, documents, papers, recommendations, or other material available to the applicable establishment which relate to programs and operations with respect to which that Inspector General has responsibilities under this Act.

There is no ambiguity in this language. IGs have access to all agency documents and information, and the legislative history to the IG Act leaves no room for doubt: the language 'all records' is expansive and is intended to include even confidential agency memoranda.[4]

## The Kate Puzey Act

Congress enacted the Kate Puzey Act following reports that emerged after the ABC network's 20/20 show aired a story on how the agency mishandled sexual assault complaints by former volunteers. The show also focused on the mishandling of an unrelated complaint filed by Kate Puzey, a volunteer who was murdered in Benin in 2009 after a staff member allegedly failed to keep her complaint confidential.[5]

Section 8E(d)(1)(B) of the Kate Puzey Act provides OIG with key oversight roles in ensuring the agency adequately responds to sexual assault and other crimes; effectively implements and trains on the Sexual Assault Risk Reduction and Response policy and program; and delivers services to sexual assault victims. The Kate Puzey Act requires that OIG conduct an evaluation on this matter and report to Congress by November 21, 2013, and again in 2016.[6] The report must be based on a case review of a statistically significant number of sexual assault cases.[7]

Section 8A(f)(2) of the Kate Puzey Act mandates that victims have access to a restricted reporting mechanism that allows them to receive services without automatically triggering an official investigation. If a victim makes a restricted report, the victim's personally identifiable information (PII) can only be shared with specified individuals unless an exception applies. One of those exceptions authorizes disclosures "to State and Federal courts when ordered, or if disclosure is required by Federal or State statute."

## Peace Corps' Legal Position

Despite the exception authorizing disclosure when required by federal law, the legal opinion asserts the exception applies only to courts because courts are the only person or organization listed in the exception. The opinion also reinterprets the statutory definition of PII in a manner that effectively prohibits OIG from accessing the crucial information it needs to fulfill its key oversight role mandated by the Kate Puzey Act.

Most egregiously, however, the opinion concludes OIG should not have access to restricted reports because the Kate Puzey Act overrides the IG Act. This is incorrect, however, since it is well established that a statute cannot be construed as overruling a pre-existing statute unless that intent is clear or the two statutes are irreconcilable.[8] Nothing in the Kate Puzey Act suggests an intent to override the IG Act and both laws can be easily reconciled by reading the exception as applying to OIG.

Furthermore, the Peace Corps' interpretation conflicts with the plain meaning of the statute as a whole.[9] The Kate Puzey Act provides OIG a central role in improving the Peace Corps' response to sexual assault victims. In particular, the law requires OIG oversee sexual assault mismanagement allegations and conduct a case review of a statistically significant number of sexual assault cases. It is inconceivable that Congress intended to increase OIG's oversight duties over the Peace Corps' response to sexual assaults, while simultaneously curtailing its ability to access the information it needs to fulfill those new duties.

## Memorandum of Understanding Between the Peace Corps and OIG

In May 2014, to avoid the possibility of remaining in the dark about a substantial category of sexual assault reports, I entered into a formal agreement with the Peace Corps granting OIG more – though not all – information from these reports, while maintaining our legal position.

The revisions the Peace Corps made to the access-denying policies and procedures as a result of the MOU are a good step forward. Since the policies and procedures were revised we have requested specific case files for two post country evaluations and have been able to review two restricted reports with corresponding redactions of PII and explicit details. However, the true test of the agreement will come this fall, when we begin reviewing a statistically significant number of cases as required by the Kate Puzey Act.

### Other Concerns

Despite the progress made – thanks in part to this Committee – I remain concerned about the appropriateness of my office having to enter into an MOU to obtain information we are entitled to by law and that we need to fulfill our statutory duties. Therefore, we see this agreement as a temporary fix to obtain information while we seek agency or congressional action.

I am also concerned the Peace Corps has yet to adequately train staff on what information can and must be shared with OIG pursuant to the MOU. There is already evidence that the Peace Corps' lack of guidance has led to staff confusion in handling sexual assaults. For example, in November we issued a management advisory report (MAR) to the Director documenting confusion on whether complaints from a third party should be treated as a restricted report.[10] The MAR documents how staff was initially advised by the Office of General Counsel not to report the information to OIG only to reverse course after discovering that other victims may have been assaulted by the same perpetrator. While the law is clear that only victims of sexual assault can make restricted reports, at least in one senior-level training the former general counsel advised staff that sexual assault allegations made by persons other than the victim should be treated as restricted and should not be reported to OIG.

Beyond training on third party complaints, staff and volunteers must be reassured that they should report allegations to our office concerning mismanagement of a sexual assault response, even if it relates to a restricted report. During the time OIG was denied access to any details of sexual assaults multiple people expressed concern about sharing information with OIG because of agency policies. Additionally, staff responsible for providing services and information to volunteers (in cases where the perpetrator is alleged to be another volunteer of staff) need to know they can consult with OIG about how our investigations are conducted, even if they are unable to provide OIG with explicit details of the assault or the victim's PII.

Finally, I am concerned about the Peace Corps' ability to meet its commitments under the agreement, such as implementing a system that would permit OIG to review sexual assault cases without full access to information. Lacking such access, Congress will be unable to properly assess whether the Peace Corps is adequately responding to victims.

## Solving the Issue

Congress and the Peace Corps have the power to solve this issue. Congress could take legislative action in one way or another to ensure we get full access to agency records.

The Peace Corps, for its part, could retract its erroneous legal opinion underlying its access-denying policies and procedures. As long as that opinion remains in place, the Peace Corps is free to rescind our agreement and withhold or delay OIG access to sexual assault reports. Moreover, its very existence sets a dangerous precedent whereby any agency may withhold information by deciding to interpret a law as overriding the IG Act.

Allowing agencies to unilaterally decide when they can or cannot release information to the IG presents a clear conflict of interest. Not only that, it forces the IG to spend its limited time and resources wrangling with the agency to obtain information – as I have done for over two years. Taxpayers – and volunteer victims of sexual assault in particular – deserve better.

While the Peace Corps withdrawing its legal opinion would resolve our access issue, it will do nothing to help other IGs who are denied full access to agency records. I appreciate the Committee's efforts to help us on our quest for access – for the sake of the Peace Corps, volunteer victims of sexual assault, and the entire IG community.

## End Notes

[1] Pub. L. No. 112-57.

[2] Pub. L. No. 113-126.

[3] On October 17, 2014, the Peace Corps issued revised Interim Policy Statement (IPS) 3-13, granting OIG access to all information from restricted reports except for the personally identifying information of volunteer victims and the explicit details of sexual assaults.

[4] S. REP. NO. 95-1071, at 33-34 (1978).

[5] The 20/20 show was not the first in-depth investigation into the underreported incidence of rape, sexual assault, and murder in the Peace Corps. On October 26, 2003, the Dayton Daily News published an article titled, "Mission of Sacrifice: Peace Corps volunteers face injury, death in foreign lands." The newspaper combed through thousands of records on volunteer assaults over a span of four decades and highlighted the alleged failings of the Peace Corps in responding to crimes against volunteers.

[6] Sec. 8E(d)(1)(A) also requires Peace Corps OIG submit a biennial report to Congress concerning reports received from volunteers that discuss incidents of misconduct, mismanagement or policy violations by Peace Corps staff, or that relate to breaches of confidentiality of volunteers.

[7] OIG submitted the initial report to Congress in November 2013 but the scope of the review did not include restricted reports because the agency had not implemented a system of restricted reporting until September 1, 2013.

[8] "The intention of the legislature to repeal must be clear and manifest." Posadas v. National City Bank of New York, 296 U.S. 497, 503 (1936). See also Tennessee Valley Authority v. Hill, 437 U.S. 153, 189–90 (1978); Morton v. Mancari, 417 U.S. 535, 549 (1974); 1 GAO, Principles of Federal Appropriations Law 2-43 (3d ed. 2004)(" A corollary to the 'cardinal

rule' against repeal by implication...is the rule of construction that statutes should be construed harmoniously so as to give maximum effect to both wherever possible.")

[9] "It is a fundamental canon of statutory construction that the words of a statute must be read in their context and with a view to their place in the overall statutory scheme... . A court must therefore interpret the statute as a symmetrical and coherent regulatory scheme, ... and fit, if possible, all parts into an harmonious whole..." FDA v. Brown and Williamson Tobacco Corp., 529 U.S. at 132–133 (citations and quotation marks omitted). See also 1 GAO, Principles of Federal Appropriations Law 2-86 (3d ed. 2004).

[10] Management Advisory Report: Agency Policies Related to volunteer Sexual Assault Allegations: http://files.peacecorps.gov/multimedia/pdf/policies/PCIG_Agency_Policies_Related_to_Volunteer_Sexual_Assault_Allegations.pdf.

In: Federal Inspectors General
Editor: Emmett Cruz
ISBN: 978-1-63485-524-2


*Chapter 8*

# STATEMENT OF WENDY GINSBERG, ANALYST IN AMERICAN NATIONAL GOVERNMENT, CONGRESSIONAL RESEARCH SERVICE. HEARING ON "STRENGTHENING GOVERNMENT OVERSIGHT: EXAMINING THE ROLES AND EFFECTIVENESS OF OVERSIGHT POSITIONS WITHIN THE FEDERAL WORKFORCE"*

Chairman Tester, Ranking Member Portman, and distinguished Members of the Subcommittee, thank you for opportunity to testify before you today on Obama Administration transparency initiatives and their effect on federal oversight.

## AN OVERVIEW OF CONGRESSIONAL OVERSIGHT

Oversight lacks a precise or consensus definition, and, in fact, is not mentioned specifically in the Constitution. Yet, oversight plays a key role in

* This is an edited, reformatted and augmented version of a statement presented November 19, 2013 before the Senate Committee on Homeland Security and Governmental Affairs, Subcommittee on the Efficiency and Effectiveness of Federal Programs and the Federal Workforce.

ensuring that our nation's laws are faithfully executed. Oversight is an implied constitutional power of Congress. On Capitol Hill, it is performed in various ways by different committees and individual Members.

One objective of oversight is to hold executive officials accountable for the execution and implementation of authorities that have been assigned or delegated to them.[1] Oversight is integral to Congress's legislative authority. It can ensure executive branch compliance with legislative intent, evaluate program performance, find efficiencies, investigate allegations of abuse or wrongdoing, assess an agency's capacity to execute its mission, ensure that executive branch policies reflect the public interest, and increase public confidence in federal programs and agencies.[2] Oversight can help ensure that the federal government is operating economically, efficiently, and effectively. Determining the appropriate quantity and quality of oversight, however, is not a simple task.

Oversight has evolved as the size of and scope of the federal government has grown.[3] Various institutional and other developments have, in some cases, limited the ability of committees and lawmakers to carry out their oversight function in a continuous fashion. For example, there are simple time and resource limitations. Oversight can require a lot of time, a deep understanding of complicated issues, and—even when performed meticulously—may not culminate in an easily measurable outcome.[4] For example, what metrics could demonstrate the utility of oversight that increased public confidence in a particular program or agency?

To meet the challenge of overseeing the execution of laws in the executive branch, Congress employs a collection of oversight tools and techniques. Among these tools and techniques are hearings and investigations; legislatively authorizing, reauthorizing or abolishing an agency's duties; the appropriations process; reporting requirements;[5] the Senate confirmation process; general management laws that require program evaluation; [6] and casework.

Additionally, Congress has enacted transparency and information access laws that provide a foundation to leverage additional oversight. Among these authorities are:

- The Administrative Procedure Act (1946);
- The Inspector General Act (1978);
- The Freedom of Information Act (1966);
- The Government Performance and Results Act (1993); and
- The E-Government Act (2002).

Congress has authorized other institutions to conduct oversight, such as its creation of the Government Accountability Office and the enactment into law of 72 federal offices of inspectors general that are authorized to find waste, fraud, and abuse.

With this summary of the oversight process, let me discuss several transparency-related efforts in both the legislative and executive branches that feature technology in a prominent way. These laws and initiatives, arguably, have changed the way federal oversight has been and can be conducted.

# I. Leveraging Technology to Enhance Data Accessibility and Increase Citizen Engagement

Advances in technology have opened up new avenues for public engagement with government. The public can watch congressional hearings in real time via committee websites, and they can contact Members and agencies through technologies that include email, Facebook, and Twitter. Access to federal databases and information has increased as a result of various legislative and executive branch initiatives. In many cases, access to accurate data can assist in making optimal policy decisions.[7] Access to information can also assist watchdog organizations, private and nonprofit entities, academics, and individual members of the public to assist in identifying issues of concern or importance to the federal government. Several examples illustrate this point.

## Obama Administration's Open Government Initiative

One particular example of an executive branch effort that builds on Congress's foundational transparency laws is President Obama's Open Government Initiative. On his first full day in office President Obama outlined this initiative, which sought to make the federal government more transparent, participatory, and collaborative.

### *The Open Government Directive*

On December 8, 2009, Peter R. Orszag, then-Director of the Office of Management and Budget (OMB), released the "Open Government Directive" memorandum, which included more detailed instructions for departments and agencies on how to "implement the principles of transparency, participation, and collaboration."[8] The memorandum required executive branch agencies to provide public, online access to "high-value" datasets that were previously unpublished.[9] Agencies were instructed to reduce their Freedom of Information Act (FOIA) backlogs by 10% per year, until they are eliminated.[10] In addition, the memorandum required each agency to designate a "high-level senior official to be accountable for the quality and objectivity of, and internal controls over, the Federal spending information" that agencies currently provide to government websites like *USAspending.gov* and *Recovery.gov*.[11] Each agency was also required to create an "open government plan ... that will describe how it will improve transparency and integrate public participation and collaboration into its activities."[12] The memorandum set a series of staggered deadlines for each department and agency to comply with the new requirements.

The directive aimed to implement the initiative's core values through four strategies:

1) Publish government information online.
2) Improve the quality of government information.
3) Create and institutionalize a culture of open government.
4) Create an enabling policy framework for open government.[13]

The Administration stated that the release of information and data would better enable the public to raise questions and keep agency performance in check—in effect, "crowdsourcing" oversight.[14]

Private sector reviews of the open government initiative have suggested that executive branch agencies met the requirements with varying levels of performance. Some agencies released thousands of datasets and created user-friendly websites, while others released minor datasets and appeared to make little attempt to create websites that offered easy access to information.[15]

***Fostering the Smart Disclosure of Federal Information***

Perhaps to address some criticism of the Open Government Directive, in 2011, OMB released another transparency-related memorandum providing guidance to agencies on releasing datasets and information that are more useful to public consumers.

The OMB guidance, entitled "Informing Consumers through Smart Disclosure,"[16] defined smart disclosure as "the timely release of complex information and data in standardized, machine readable formats ... that enable consumers to make informed decisions." Smart disclosure, the memorandum continued, requires that data are accessible, machine readable,[17] standardized,[18] timely, adaptive to markets and innovation,[19] interoperable,[20] and protective of individuals' privacy.[21] Pursuant to the guidance, agencies were to determine "whether and how to best promote smart disclosure."[22] In May 2013, the federal Task Force on Smart Disclosure further detailed recommendations for implementation.[23] Among these recommendations were making federal agency data systems interoperable with other systems within and outside of individual agencies; ensuring that aggregated databases that are released to the public cannot be mined to inappropriately release sensitive information about individuals; and hosting code-a-thons and workshops that can assist in the development and demonstration of new ways to use existing datasets.[24]

## The Creation of Recovery.gov

Another transparency-related oversight mechanism was the establishment of *Recovery.gov* in compliance with the American Recovery and Reinvestment Act of 2009 (ARRA; P.L. 111-5).[25] The website was intended to be a repository for information related to implementation and oversight of ARRA funding. The website currently includes overview information about the legislation, accountability reports and actions, frequently asked questions, and data on the distribution of funds and major recipients.

*Recovery.gov* was built by the Recovery Accountability and Transparency Board (RATB), a committee of inspectors general from around the federal government. The public-facing website arguably allowed "taxpayers to be in a better position to hold their government accountable."[26] While the website initially contained inaccurate information, the RATB enforced policies to remedy these errors.[27] Additionally, the federal government used the website to make public the names of those funding recipients who failed to appropriately file spending and job creation data. It is unclear, however, whether the public release of these recipients' names prompted greater compliance with federal law,[28] or whether the website increased accountability of participating agency and funding recipients.

Congress and the President have engaged in several additional initiatives that use technology to create public-facing databases that seek to use "crowdsourcing" to assist in federal oversight. Among the examples are *USASpending.gov*;[29] *Data.gov*;[30] and *Performance.gov*.[31]

# II. Opportunities and Challenges for Inspectors General — Balancing Information Access with Privacy and Security

Increasing use of technology and the Internet, which has accompanied greater access to federal government records and operations, is often in tension with the protection of information from inappropriate release.[32]

As noted earlier, transparency and access can help promote an informed citizenry. Yet America's lawmakers have enacted into law certain categories of information and records that can or must be protected from public release. For example, FOIA protects information that if released could harm national security, invade someone's personal privacy, or hinder an ongoing criminal investigation.[33] Members of the federal government's oversight workforce often have to balance these tensions between access and protection.

## Advances in Technology and Oversight by Inspectors General

Since 1978, Congress has authorized federal inspectors general to serve as permanent, independent, and nonpartisan units that combat waste, fraud, and abuse in the federal government (5 U.S.C. Appendix).[34] These 72 offices are using technology in a variety of ways to assist congressional oversight and make the government more effective and efficient. Three principal purposes or missions guide the offices of inspector general (OIGs):

- conduct and supervise audits and investigations relating to the programs and operations of the applicable agency;
- provide leadership and coordination and recommend policies for activities designed to (1) promote economy, efficiency, and effectiveness in the administration of such programs and operations; and (2) prevent and detect fraud and abuse in such programs and operations; and
- provide a means for keeping the head of the applicable agency and Congress fully and currently informed about problems and deficiencies relating to the administration of such programs and operations, as well as the necessity for and progress of corrective action.[35]

Such offices now exist in all Cabinet departments, many federal agencies, as well as many boards, commissions, government corporations, and foundations.

The overwhelming majority of OIGs are governed by the Inspector General Act of 1978, as amended (hereinafter referred to as the IG Act),[36] which has been substantially modified twice as well as subject to agency-specific OIG amendments.[37] The IG Act structured appointments and removals, powers and authorities, and responsibilities and duties.[38]

An OIG, depending upon its associated agency's mission, can perform oversight of internal operations or external outputs. For example, in 2009, the inspector general at the Department of Health and Human Services (the federal department charged with administering Medicare, Medicaid, and other federal healthcare programs) reportedly devoted 85% of the office's resources to reducing or preventing fraud involving healthcare program providers.[39] In contrast, that same year the Department of Homeland Security OIG (which oversees an entity with jurisdiction over a variety of agencies, including the U.S. Citizenship and Immigration Service and U.S. Customs and Border Protection) reportedly allocated 75% of the office's resources to oversight and investigations of internal operations, even though roughly 50% of the Department's resources were spent on grants and outside contracts.[40]

The vast differences in agency missions, and, therefore, OIG oversight of the agencies' missions and priorities, may lead to disparate adoption of the use of technology within the OIG community. According to a September 2011 survey conducted by the Council on Inspectors General for Integrity and Efficiency's (CIGIE's) New Media Working Group, only 26 of more than 70 OIGs reported using any form of "new media."[41] One recent publication found that social media can assist OIGs in gathering information for investigations[42] and can help keep OIGs informed about news stories, agency actions, the findings of "citizen reporters," and priorities of their congressional overseers.[43] Moreover, new media can help OIGs comply with the Open Government Initiative to disseminate their own information, reports, and findings.[44]

In addition to new media technologies, OIGs may benefit from the use of IT to create additional efficiencies. For example, OIGs can use online databases and information to assist their audits and investigations. If OIGs are charged with finding agency waste, fraud, and abuse in all realms, then training and awareness of online databases, online scams, and use of social media may be necessary.

As was discussed at a series of meetings on the potential applications and complications of data analytics for oversight and law enforcement, most federal information technology (IT) systems are often designed to execute a specific program or mission, such as automate the distribution of a particular federal benefit. The IT system may not be designed to assist in determining the enforcement of eligibility requirements for the benefit program or to identify other program vulnerabilities.[45] By not incorporating the future needs of oversight officials in the design of new IT systems, some modernization efforts may limit the ability of IGs and others to use data to uncover waste, fraud, and abuse. In addition, overseers may attempt to use available data in ways that were not "originally intended, which can create challenges."[46]

OIGs may choose not to embrace all technologies. CIGIE's new media working group, for example, recommends that each OIG measure whether the benefits of a particular technology are worth its accompanying costs "based on IT resources and mission."[47]

## The Challenges of Leveraging Technology

As OIGs and other oversight entities begin or continue to adopt evolving technologies, the protection of sensitive information and the creation of policies and procedures for appropriate use of IT will be of continuing concern.[48] Technology and new media can prompt complexities in information security,[49] privacy,[50] legal oversight,[51] and records collection.[52]

Continued use of large databases and new media may require investments in training, equipment, personnel, and other resources. Additionally, existing statutes, regulations, or policies may need to be revisited to determine whether they encumber IGs, the public, and other entities from effectively using online tools and data to assist oversight. For example, in a July 2013 document highlighting the findings of an earlier forum, GAO noted that "participants from the IG community" voiced concerns over a component of the Privacy Act (5 U.S.C. § 552a), as amended, that requires certain notification procedures in cases when automated data systems are shared between federal agencies or between a federal agency and a non-federal agency.[53] Specifically, the Computer Matching and Privacy Protection Act of 1988 (P.L. 100-503; 5 U.S.C § 552a), as amended, requires agencies to draft a written agreement about the use, purpose, and intended protections of any qualifying electronic system of records before it can be shared. Such sharing of datasets may assist overseers in proactively discovering fraudulent or incorrect applications for federal assistance or contracts—thereby, increasing program integrity.

For the purposes of the Privacy Act, OIGs are considered a separate agency from the agency or department they are authorized to audit and investigate. The Privacy Act, therefore, appears to require OIGs and any applicable agencies to draft agreements for sharing of electronic systems of records. According to members of the OIG community, these agreements can take years to complete.[54] Participants at the forum noted that the act may "threaten the principle of independence," which is codified in the Inspector General Act (5 U.S.C. Appendix). This component of the Privacy Act has been identified as a potential difficulty for the IG community since at least 1998, when the chairperson of the President's Council on Integrity and Efficiency (the precursor of CIGIE) testified before the House Committee on Government Reform and Oversight in favor of legislation that would permit certain federal agencies to match benefit applications to electronic data owned by the Internal Revenue Service.[55]

## III. Transparency Initiatives Can Strengthen Accountability, But Do Not Substitute for Other Oversight Mechanisms

Online databases and new media can allow OIGs and the public to take part in the Administration's stated commitment of being more transparent and participatory. Making information available to the public and to OIGs is, arguably, not an end in itself. Although data and information can contribute to a more informed citizenry and a more efficient government, the constitutionally-established structure of the U.S. government authorizes certain elected and appointed federal officials—not the public and not OIGs—to determine and execute federal policy. OIGs,[56] GAO, and other oversight mechanisms are empowered to publish their findings, research, and recommendations—but not to enforce the adoption of recommended policies. Instead, information access, if operationalized effectively, may aid stakeholders and the public in holding the federal government more accountable for its actions or inactions and prompt debates on how to make the government operate more efficiently and effectively.

Making vast amounts of data available to the public is not the same as oversight. For data and information to become helpful in federal oversight, they, arguably, must be appropriately used, clearly stated, and the results must be presented fairly. In some cases, data and analytics may not be the optimal oversight tools. Conducting personal interviews, working with whistleblowers, and site visits may remain the most effective courses of action in these cases.

Technology can assist in government oversight. It can provide new information and allow overseers to use data in innovative ways. Technology and use of new media can assist in investigations and facilitate public input on agency actions.[57] Providing interested stakeholders access to information can allow them to track where federal dollars are spent, can provide context on the methodology used to rate the most effective child safety seat, or can provide data on the spread of the flu virus. This access may help uncover fraud, improve safety, or even save lives. Technology, however, must be thoughtfully employed and sensitive data and information must remain protected.

Access to information alone, however, is not the equivalent of oversight. Oversight also involves the analysis of agency actions to evaluate economy, efficiency, and effectiveness. Moreover, public interest in oversight is not inherently uniform across issues or consistent over time. As a result, although transparency initiatives may facilitate citizen engagement in highly visible issues, it is less clear whether such initiatives encourage comparable participation in more routine oversight.

Access to information and federal datasets may enable scholars to access and analyze information and create new tools to show how government operates. To make “crowdsourcing” technologies relevant to federal oversight, however, agencies need to ensure that datasets released to the public or made available to OIGs are authoritative. Agencies may need to clarify any limitations of the data—for example, are some populations underrepresented in a dataset, or are there particular data points that may skew the data toward more extreme averages—so users are not inadvertently misled when analyzing the data.

As agencies release hundreds or thousands of datasets or vast amounts of records, users may need specialized knowledge to identify appropriate information to meet their needs. Counterintuitively, the release of data and records can decrease executive branch transparency, and, perhaps, hinder oversight. For example, users may have to sift through thousands of datasets to determine which ones include the information they seek. It may be difficult for a researcher to pinpoint the records he or she needs in a collection of similarly titled datasets. Other data may be made available in a format with which a researcher is unfamiliar.

Oversight can be performed using a variety of tools, techniques, and institutions. The release of new datasets and the use of new media can create new opportunities for oversight, can assist investigations, and can allow interested members of the public to share in working toward a more effective and efficient government. Technology, however, is not without costs. Monetary costs would include purchasing software and equipment, hiring employees who can use the technology, and training employees to keep up with evolving technologies. Non-monetary costs may include a greater risk of an information security breach, unintentional release of sensitive information, or increased challenges in meeting the requirements of particular federal laws—such as records management laws.[58]

Despite these costs and potential risks, CIGIE's New Media Working Group encourages agencies to thoughtfully and carefully embrace IT and new media. As the working group asserts, simply blocking the use of new media "does not eliminate information security threats."[59] Moreover, if crimes, ethical violations, and inefficiencies occur online, investigators and auditors will need to build their own capacity in use of IT to perform their oversight functions. Planning the implementation and use policies of IT and new media prior to their dissemination can prevent unwanted or improper releases of individuals' private information and make clear to employees the appropriate applications of the technologies. Evolving technologies may also prompt the need for Congress to reexamine existing records management and records protection statutes to ensure that they protect sensitive information appropriately and that they permit access to information that can assist in all forms of federal oversight.

## CONCLUDING REMARKS

Congressional oversight is a vital component of an effective and efficient federal government. Woodrow Wilson, former president and political scientist, wrote in his 1885 research on the legislative branch

> Unless Congress have and use every means of acquainting itself with the acts and dispositions of the administrative agency of the government, the country must be helpless to learn how it is being served; and unless Congress both scrutinize these things and sift them by every form of discussion, the country must remain in embarrassing, crippling ignorance of the very affairs which it is most important it should understand and direct.

Mr. Chairman, this concludes my opening statement. Thank you again for the opportunity to testify, and I look forward to the Subcommittee's questions.

## End Notes

[1] For additional information on congressional oversight, generally, see CRS Report R41079, *Congressional Oversight: An Overview*, by Walter J. Oleszek.

[2] CRS Report RL30240, *Congressional Oversight Manual*, by Todd Garvey et al.

[3] For example, the so-called modern era of government has witnessed authorization for and creation of a "presidential branch" of government (the Office of Management and Budget, the National Security Council, and the like) and the establishment of many federal departments and agencies. From three departments in 1789 (State, Treasury, and War, renamed Defense in 1947), a dozen more have been added to the cabinet. The newest creation, in 2002, is the Department of Homeland Security (DHS). Formed from the merger of 22 separate executive branch units, it employees roughly 180,000 people. Other scholars have referred to the growth of the executive branch as "the administrative state." See Lawrence C. Dodd and Richard L. Schott, *Congress and the Administrative State* (New York: John Wiley and Sons, 1979).

[4] See, for example, the statement of a Senator in *Congress Speaks: A Survey of the 100th Congress* (Washington, DC: Center for Responsive Politics, 1988), p. 163.

[5] For more information on reporting requirements, see CRS Report R42490, *Reexamination of Agency Reporting Requirements: Annual Process Under the GPRA Modernization Act of 2010 (GPRAMA)*, by Clinton T. Brass.

[6] For more on the authorities created by Congress to promote transparency and public oversight, see CRS Report R42817, *Government Transparency and Secrecy: An Examination of Meaning and Its Use in the Executive Branch*, by Wendy Ginsberg et al.

[7] *Government Transparency: Efforts to Improve Information on Federal Spending*, GAO-12-913T, July 18, 2012, pp. 11; and Partnership for Public Service, *From Data to Decisions II: Building an Analytics Culture*, October 2012, pp. 10-12.

[8] Executive Office of the President, Office of Management and Budget, *Memorandum for the Heads of Executive Departments and Agencies: Open Government Directive*, December 8, 2009, at http://www.whitehouse.gov/omb/assets/memoranda_2010/ m10-06.pdf.

[9] An attachment to the memorandum provided a definition of what would qualify as a "high value data set," stating "[h]igh value information is information that can be used to increase agency accountability and responsiveness; improve public knowledge of the agency and its operations; further the core mission of the agency; create economic opportunity; or respond to need and demand as identified through public consultation." Executive Office of the President, Office of Management and Budget, *Memorandum for the Heads of Executive Departments and Agencies: Open Government Directive*, December 8, 2009, Attachment, pp. 7-8.

[10] FOIA (5 U.S.C. § 552) provides the public presumed access to executive branch agency records. For more information on FOIA and particular categories of records that are exempted from public release, see CRS Report R41933, *The Freedom of Information Act (FOIA): Background and Policy Options for the 113th Congress*, by Wendy Ginsberg.

[11] Ibid., p. 3.

[12] Ibid., p. 4.

[13] Executive Office of the President, Office of Management and Budget, *Memorandum for the Heads of Executive Departments and Agencies: Open Government Directive*, Washington, DC, December 8, 2009.

[14] At a December 10, 2009, Senate Budget Committee Task Force on Government Performance hearing, both the federal CIO (then Vivek Kundra) and the federal CTO (then Aneesh Chopra) said that watch dog groups and members of the public would enforce agency accountability. U.S. Congress, Senate Committee on the Budget, Task Force on Government Performance, *Data-Driven Performance: Using Technology to Deliver Results*, 111th Congress, 1st session, December 10, 2009, at http://www.senate.gov/fplayers/CommPlayer/commFlashPlayer.cfm?fn=budget121009&st=1005.

[15] One private entity's examination of the OGD was OMB Watch's (now known as The Center for Effective Government), "Leaders and Laggards in Agency Open Government Webpages," February 23, 2010, at http://www.foreffectivegov.org/node/10785/. OMB Watch also wrote a similarly mixed review follow-up assessment of the Open Government Directive, "OMB Watch Assesses Obama Administration's Progress on Open Government Recommendations," March 18, 2011, at http://www.foreffectivegov.org/node/11558. The Sunlight Foundation noted that many agencies met the requirements of the directive, but did not execute particular initiatives they had planned to accomplish. See The Sunlight Foundation, "Obama's Open Government Directive, Two Years On," December 7, 2011, at http://sunlightfoundation.com/blog/2011/12/07/obamas-open-government-directive-two-years-on/. *The Michigan Journal of Environmental and Administrative Law* also published an online blog post noting the mixed results of the directive and encouraged the President to continue make transparency a priority. See Eric Merron, *Michigan Journal of Environmental and Administrative Law*, "Obama's Open Government Initiative: A Progress Report," February 24, 2013, at http://students.law.umich.edu/mjeal/2013/02/obama%E2%80%99s-open-government-initiative-progress-report/.

[16] Cass R. Sunstein, *Informing Consumers through Smart Disclosure*, Office of Management and Budget, Washington, DC, September 8, 2011, at http://www.whitehouse.gov/sites/default/files/omb/inforeg/for-agencies/informing-consumers-throughsmart-disclosure.pdf.

[17] Pursuant to the memorandum, machine readable means the data are "stored in a format enabling the information to be process and analyzed by computer," for example, formats that could be "readily imported into spreadsheet and database applications." Ibid., p. 5.

[18] Pursuant to the memorandum, standardization requires that information "be available in standardized vocabularies and formats ... that allow for meaningful comparisons and other analyses across datasets." (Ibid.)

[19] Pursuant to the memorandum, market adaptation and innovation would require agencies to "periodically consult with user communities ... to review and adapt smart disclosure regimes so that the information conveyed remains accurate and relevant." Ibid. p. 6.

[20] Pursuant to the memorandum, interoperable means that the data are more valuable if they "can be linked to other sources of data" through "common identifiers ... using consistent vocabulary."(Ibid.)

[21] Ibid, pp. 5-6.

[22] Ibid., p. 2.

[23] National Science and Technology Council, "Smart Disclosure and Consumer Decision Making: Report of the Task Force on Smart Disclosure," May 2013, at http://www.whitehouse.gov/sites/default/files/microsites/ostp/report_of_the_task_force_on_smart_disclosure.pdf.

[24] Ibid., pp. 22-25.

[25] CRS Report R40572, *General Oversight Provisions in the American Recovery and Reinvestment Act of 2009 (ARRA): Requirements and Related Issues* by Clinton T. Brass.

[26] Michael F. Wood and Alice M Siempelkamp, "Transparency in Government," *The Journal of Public Inquiry*, Fall/Winter 2010/2011, p. 2.

[27] U.S. Government Accountability Office, *Government Transparency: Efforts to Improve Information on Federal Spending*, GAO-12-913T, July 18, 2012, pp. 8-9, at http://gao.gov/assets/600/592592.pdf.

[28] See, for example, Michael Wood, *Recovery Blog*, Recovery Board, Shaming the Scofflaws, Washington, DC, March 28, 2012, http://blog.recovery.gov/2012/03/28/shaming-the-scofflaws/.

[29] *USASpending.gov* was established as a component of the Federal Funding and Accountability and Transparency Act of 2006 (P.L. 109-282). It provides information about federal contract and grant awards. For more on USASpending.gov, see CRS Report R42769, *Federal Grants-in-Aid Administration: A Primer*, by Natalie Keegan.

[30] *Data.gov* is an Obama Administration initiative that encourages agencies to proactively release federal datasets to the public. For more on Data.gov and transparency, see CRS Report R42817, *Government Transparency and Secrecy: An Examination of Meaning and Its Use in the Executive Branch*, by Wendy Ginsberg et al.

[31] *Performance.gov* was established as a component of the GPRA Modernization Act of 2010 (GPRAMA; P.L. 111-35). The website provides information about executive agency goals, measures, and programs. for more information on GPRAMA, see CRS Report R42379, *Changes to the Government Performance and Results Act (GPRA): Overview of the New Framework of Products and Processes*, by Clinton T. Brass.

[32] Although transparency and information protection are often discussed as being in tension, it has been argued that government openness can lead to better national security. See Thomas S. Blanton, "National Security and Open Government in the United States: Beyond the Balancing Test," in Suzanne Piotrowski, *Transparency and Secrecy: A Reader Linking Literature and Contemporary Debate*, (Lanham, MD: Lexington Books, 2010), p. 26.

[33] CRS Report R41933, *The Freedom of Information Act (FOIA): Background and Policy Options for the 113th Congress*, by Wendy Ginsberg.

[34] In addition to statutory inspectors general, other temporary and permanent inspectors general or watchdog-type organizations exist across the federal government. Some of these offices include the Government Accountability Office (GAO), which describes itself as "an independent, nonpartisan agency that works for Congress ... and investigates how the federal government spends taxpayer dollars." Additionally, a variety of federal agencies have federal ombudsmen who may assist employees internally with workforce concerns or assist the public with operational or other concerns. For more information on federal ombudsmen, see CRS Report RL34606, *Federal Complaint-Handling, Ombudsman, and Advocacy Offices*, by Wendy Ginsberg and Frederick M. Kaiser.

[35] 5 U.S.C. Appendix, § 2.

[36] 5 U.S.C. Appendix.

[37] The Inspector General Act Amendments of 1988 created a new set of IGs in "designated federal entities" (DFEs), which are usually found among smaller federal agencies, and added to the reporting obligations of all IGs and agency heads, among other things.[37] The Inspector General Reform Act of 2008 established a new Council of the Inspectors General for Integrity and Efficiency (CIGIE); amended reporting obligations, salary and bonus

provisions, and removal requirements; and added certain budget protections for offices of inspector general.

[38] P.L. 95-452.

[39] Project on Government Oversight, *Inspectors General: Accountability is a Balancing Act*, Washington, DC, March 20, 2009, p. 23, at http://www.pogo.org/our-work/reports/2009/go-igi-20090320.html.

[40] Ibid., p. 24.

[41] Department of Homeland Security Office of Inspector General on behalf of the Council of the Inspectors General on Integrity and Efficiency's New Media Working Group, *Recommended Practices for Office of Inspectors General Use of New Media*, Washington, DC, September 2011, pp. 3-4, at http://www.ignet.gov/randp/cigienewmediarpt1111.pdf. The report defined "new media" as encompassing "all forms of electronic, digitalized, and interactive media, including tools that allow interactive communication with an external audience and those used solely internally." (Ibid. p. 6). Among the tools included within the working group's definition of new media were SharePoint, Wiki, audio or video podcasts, blogs, Facebook, LinkedIn, RSS Feed, Twitter, and YouTube. (Ibid., pp. 6-7).

[42] Nancy Eyl, "What Social Media Has to Offer Offices of Inspectors General," *Journal of Public Inquiry*, Fall/Winter 2012/2013, p. 21. Use of social media as an investigation tool can "establish motives, prove and disprove alibis ... provide leads" and help establish a subject's social circle. (Ibid.).

[43] Ibid. See also CRS Report R43018, *Social Networking and Constituent Communications: Members' Use of Twitter and Facebook During a Two-Month Period in the 112th Congress*, by Matthew E. Glassman, Jacob R. Straus, and Colleen J. Shogan, which analyzes congressional use of Twitter by Members of Congress. Using social media like Twitter, could allow OIGs to communicate their work to Members as well as for OIGs to better understand the priorities of their congressional overseers. See also, U.S. Government Accountability Office, *Social Media: Federal Agencies Need Policies and Procedures for Managing and Protecting Information They Access and Disseminate*, GAO-11-605, June 2011, at http://www.gao.gov/assets/330/320244.pdf.

[44] Nancy Eyl, "What Social Media Has to Offer Offices of Inspectors General," *Journal of Public Inquiry,* p. 22. OIGs, for example, could educate the public "about waste, fraud, and abuse," "increase appropriate hotline use," and "help OIGs control the message about the work they do." (Ibid.)

[45] U.S. Government Accountability Office, *Highlights of a Forum: Data Analytics For Oversight and Law Enforcement*, GAO13-680SP, July 2013, p. 4, at http://www.gao.gov/assets/660/655871.pdf.

[46] Ibid.

[47] Department of Homeland Security Office of Inspector General on behalf of the Council of the Inspectors General on Integrity and Efficiency's New Media Working Group, *Recommended Practices for Office of Inspectors General Use of New Media*, Washington, DC, September 2011, p. 18, at http://www.ignet.gov/randp/cigienewmediarpt1111.pdf.

[48] U.S. Government Accountability Office, *Social Media: Federal Agencies Need Policies and Procedures for Managing and Protecting Information They Access and Disseminate*, GAO-11-605, June 2011, at http://www.gao.gov/assets/330/320244.pdf.

[49] Information security requirements are authorized in the Federal Information Security Management Act of 2002 (FISMA; 44 U.S.C. §§ 3541-3549). For an overview of FISMA, see CRS Report R42114, *Federal Laws Relating to Cybersecurity: Overview and Discussion of Proposed Revisions*, by Eric A. Fischer.

[50] The primary authority addressing the protection of personal privacy is the Privacy Act of 1974, amended (5 U.S.C. § 552a).

[51] Legal oversight relates to the legal requirements and policies associated with the use of particular new media. General Services Administration (GSA) leads a coalition of federal agencies that created "federal-compatible terms of service (TOS)" for use of social media tools that are offered for use from particular private vendors. See HowTo.gov, "Federal-Compatible Terms of Service Agreements," at http://www.howto.gov/social-media/terms-of-service-agreements. OIGs and other federal agencies can use these TOS documents as templates and use their in-house legal oversight to amend the service agreement to better fit the individual needs of their agency.

[52] Federal records collection, retention, and maintenance are authorized in the Federal Records Act (44 U.S.C. Chapters 21, 29, 31, and 33). For more information on how technology is affecting records collection and retention, see CRS Report R43165, *Retaining and Preserving Federal Records in a Digital Environment: Background and Issues for Congress*, by Wendy Ginsberg.

[53] GAO, Data Analytics, GAO-13-680SP.

[54] GAO, Data Analytics, GAO-13-680SP, p. 11. Other participants at the forum noted that the law may prohibit a sharing of the database itself, but did not prohibit agencies from sharing hardcopies of the same information.

[55] U.S. Congress, House Committee on Government Reform and Oversight, Subcommittee on Government Management, Information, and Technology, Hearing on H.R. 4243, H.R. 2347; and H.R. 2063, 105th Congress, 2nd session, March 2, 1998, H.Hrg. 105-143 (Washington: GPO, 1998), pp. 103-104.

[56] Pursuant to 5 U.S.C. Appendix § 3(c), "no Inspector General shall be considered to be an employee who determines policies to be pursued by the United States in the nationwide administration of Federal laws."

[57] Beth Simone Noveck, *Wiki Government: How Technology Can Make Government Better, Democracy Stronger, and Citizens More Powerful* (Washington, DC: Brookings Institution Press, 2010).

[58] CRS Report R43165, *Retaining and Preserving Federal Records in a Digital Environment: Background and Issues for Congress*, by Wendy Ginsberg.

[59] Department of Homeland Security Office of Inspector General on behalf of the Council of the Inspectors General on Integrity and Efficiency's New Media Working Group, *Recommended Practices for Office of Inspectors General Use of New Media*, p. 17.

# INDEX

## G



## H



## I

## J



## L



## M



## N



## O



## P

## R



## S



## T

## U



## V



## W